Communications in Computer and Information Science 627

Commenced Publication in 2007
Founding and Former Series Editors:
Alfredo Cuzzocrea, Dominik Ślęzak, and Xiaokang Yang

More information about this series at http://www.springer.com/series/7899

B. Vinod · Richard Voyles
Prahlad Vadakkepat · M. Sundaram
K.S. Sujatha · J. Joe Brislin (Eds.)

Advancements in Automation, Robotics and Sensing

First International Conference, ICAARS 2016
Coimbatore, India, June 23–24, 2016
Revised Selected Papers

 Springer

Editors

B. Vinod
Department of Robotics and Automation
  Engineering
PSG College of Technology
Coimbatore
India

Richard Voyles
College of Technology
Purdue University
Lafayette, IN
USA

Prahlad Vadakkepat
Electrical and Computer Engineering
National University of Singapore
Singapore
Singapore

M. Sundaram
Department of Robotics and Automation
  Engineering
PSG College of Technology
Coimbatore
India

K.S. Sujatha
Department of Robotics and Automation
  Engineering
PSG College of Technology
Coimbatore
India

J. Joe Brislin
Department of Robotics and Automation
  Engineering
PSG College of Technology
Coimbatore
India

ISSN 1865-0929   ISSN 1865-0937 (electronic)
Communications in Computer and Information Science
ISBN 978-981-10-2844-1   ISBN 978-981-10-2845-8   (eBook)
DOI 10.1007/978-981-10-2845-8

Library of Congress Control Number: 2016954197

Printed on acid-free paper

This Springer imprint is published by Springer Nature
The registered company is Springer Nature Singapore Pte Ltd.
The registered company address is: 152 Beach Road, #22-06/08 Gateway East, Singapore 189721, Singapore

Preface

The First International Conference on Advancements in Automation, Robotics, and Sensing (ICAARS 2016) was held in Coimbatore, India, by the Department of Robotics and Automation Engineering, PSG College of Technology, during June 23–24 2016. As the name suggests, it aims at the convergence of three fields, acting as a common forum for the robotics and automation research communities. This year's conference had a special focus on developments in sensors, imaging systems, adaptive control systems, and design and deployment of manipulators for various remote material handling systems contributing to advancements in the field of robotics and industrial automation. The conference hosted in India provided ample opportunity for participants from all over the world to form professional networks and learn through active participation. Nine intriguing keynotes from academia and industry complemented the technical program. We would like to thank everybody who contributed to the success of this conference, in particular the members of the technical committee and the additional reviewers for carefully reviewing the contributions. To add value to the conference, a pre-conference workshop was conducted by bringing together researchers from academia and industry, for the fostering of collaboration and exchange of ideas. The pre-conference workshop chair, Dr. Richard Voyles, Associate Dean for Research, Purdue University, USA, excelled in organizing the tutorials and coordinating the workshop. We thank Dr. R. Rudramoorthy, Principal, and the management of PSG College of Technology for giving us a platform to conduct such a wonderful and successful event. Our special thanks to the members of the Organizing Committee for their numerous contributions. We hope that all participants enjoyed a successful conference, made many new contacts, engaged in fruitful discussions, and had a pleasant stay in Coimbatore.

September 2016   B. Vinod

Organization

Advisory Board

Richard Voyles	Purdue University, USA
Dong-Soo Kwon	KAIST, Korea
Vijay Kumar	University of Pennsylvania, USA
Ewald Bentz	Lapp Group, Germany
Prahlad Vadakkepat	NUS, Singapore
Robert Doornick	International Robotics Inc., USA
Balan Pillai	Stanford University, USA
Raj Rajkumar	Carnegie Mellon University, USA
Ravi Balasubramanian	Oregon State University, USA
Dirk Frohling	Westfalische Hochschule, Germany
Swami Vangal Ramamurthy	Adept, Singapore
Baldevraj	NIAS, India
G.C. Nandi	IIIT Allahabad, India
Prabir K. Pal	DRHR, BARC, India
D.N. Badodkar	BARC, India
Swarna Ramesh	CVRDE, India
Ashish Dutta	IITK, India
Asokan Thondiyath	IITM, India
R. Krishnamoorthy	L&T Technologies, India
S. Paramasivam	Danfoss, India
S. Murugan	IGCAR, India

Convener

B. Vinod	PSG College of Technology, India

Co-convener

A.R. Ramakrishnan	PSG College of Technology, India

Organizing Secretary(s)

M. Sundaram	PSG College of Technology, India
K.S. Sujatha	PSG College of Technology, India

Finance Chair

C.S. Sundar Ganesh	PSG College of Technology, India

Workshop Chair

T. Subramani   PSG College of Technology, India

Hospitality and Exhibition Chair

S. Prabhakaran   PSG College of Technology, India

Proceedings Chair

J. Joe Brislin   PSG College of Technology, India

Web Chair

R. Gowri   PSG College of Technology, India

Steering Committee

M. Vasanthakumar   PSG College of Technology, India
B. Bindu   PSG College of Technology, India
V. Vishwa Priya   PSG College of Technology, India
A. Sivaranjani   PSG College of Technology, India

Session Chairs

Richard Voyles   Purdue University, USA
Balan Pillai   Stanford University, USA
Dirk Frohling   Westfalische Hochschule, Germany
Rajan Pillai   Nesta Group, India
Akshay Nagarajan   Ammachi Labs, India
Vijayavel Bagavath Singh   EFESTO, USA
Pranay Kishore   Phi robotics, India
S. Vishwesh   SVP Laser Technologies, India
A.P. Sudheer   NIT Calicut, India
Rajam Ramaswamy   Coimbatore Institute of Technology, India
E. Chandirasekar   Coimbatore Institute of Technology, India
P. Ganeshan   PSGIAS, India
K.K. Venkatraman   PSGIAS, India
J. Kanchana   PSGIAS, India
Ila Venila   PSG College of Technology, India

Contents

Remote Material Handling Systems

A Customized Servo Manipulator for Remote Handling in Nuclear Facilities

M.N. Rao[1](✉), S. Panda[1], R.V. Sakrikar[1], Tumapala Teja Swaroop[1], Debasish Datta Ray[1], and K. Jayarajan[2]

[1] DRHR, BARC, Trombay, Mumbai 400085, India
mnrao@barc.gov.in
[2] BSCS, BARC, Trombay, Mumbai 400085, India

Abstract. Radioactivity is an inevitable problem in nuclear industry. Therefore, radioactive materials are handled remotely, using remote handling tools, such as Master Slave Manipulators. Bhabha Atomic Research Centre (BARC), Mumbai has recently developed a Customized Servo Manipulator (CSM), for use in radioactive areas, which cannot be accessible by conventional manipulators. All joints and the gripper on slave arm are electrically driven. The master arm is a scaled down version of the slave arm and is provided with the necessary sensors for master-slave operations.

Keywords: Radioactivity · Remote handling · Manipulators

1 Introduction

Master Slave Manipulators (MSMs) [1] are the most dexterous general-purpose remote handling tools in nuclear industry. An MSM has two arms: a master arm in the operating area and a slave arm in the hotcell. When the human operator holds and manipulates the master arm, the gripper in slave arm reproduces the motion of the handgrip in the master arm. Based on the mechanical power source, MSMs are classified as mechanical manipulators and servo manipulators: mechanical manipulators use the power of the human operator, whereas the servo manipulators use electric or hydraulic actuators.

1.1 Mechanical Manipulators

In a mechanical manipulator, the master arm and the slave arm are mechanically coupled by a through-tube in the wall-sleeve of the radioactive cell (hotcell). It is a complex mechanism with 6 to 9 ° of freedom. The motions generated by the operator on the master arm are mechanically transmitted to the slave arm, through the linkages in the master arm, the through-tube and the slave arm.

Various models of mechanical manipulators, with range of payload from 1 kg to 45 kg, reach from 1 m to 3 m and varied power transmission techniques, have been designed and deployed in large numbers in different units of Department of Atomic Energy (DAE). Wire ropes and chains are used in the Articulated Manipulator models,

© Springer Nature Singapore Pte Ltd. 2016
B. Vinod et al. (Eds.): ICAARS 2016, CCIS 627, pp. 3–10, 2016.
DOI: 10.1007/978-981-10-2845-8_1

whereas the models like MSM, Extended Reach Manipulator (ERM), Rugged Duty Manipulator (RDM) and Three-Piece Manipulator (TPM) [2] use tapes, shafts, etc. for power transmission between the master and the slave arms.

1.2 Servo Manipulators

In the servo manipulator, the master arm and the slave arm are not mechanically coupled: they are connected through electric cables through a controller. It gives flexibility to the slave arm for mounting it on a transporter in the hotcell, giving large effective range. In a mechanical manipulator, force and energy for performing a task have to be provided by the human operator, whereas in servo manipulators they are provided by an external power source, making the later more operator-friendly. Two models of the servo manipulators, Mark-I and Mark-II have been developed. Two pairs of servo manipulators (Mark-I) are installed in a hotcell for vitrification of nuclear waste. The Advanced Servo Manipulator (Mark-II) [3], with digital distributed controls and force reflection, has many advanced operator friendly features.

We have recently developed a Force Reflecting Telerobot [4], an upgraded version of the Advanced Servo Manipulator. In addition to master following mode, the slave arm can also be controlled as a robot through a computer. The force reflecting telerobot represents a new generation of remote handling tool, with advanced features like position control of the slave arm in world coordinates, indexing in world coordinates, scaling of slave motion, constrained motion, teach & playback and interactive robot control.

Although, servo manipulator offers many superior features over their mechanical counter parts, they cannot be installed in the existing hotcells, due to the lack of a mounting structure in these cells. Our experience in developing TPM and Servo Manipulators led us to the development of Four-Piece Servo Manipulator (FPSM) [5], which can be installed through the wall sleeves of hotcells. FPSM has the advantage of low friction compared to the inherent high friction in TPMs. FPSM would offer maintainability of TPM and ease of operation of Servo Manipulators.

The experience gained during the development of the servo manipulators have led to the design and development of a Customized Servo Manipulator suitable for inaccessible radioactive areas.

2 Mechanical Design of CSM

The CSM being consists of a master arm and a slave arm, which are coupled with each other electrically. The CSM slave arm is designed for payload of 3 kg and reach of 1 m. It is provided with electrically operated, positive locking gripper. The master and the slave arm are linked together by a suitable control system for its operations. Figures 1 and 2 show the slave and master arms of CSM.

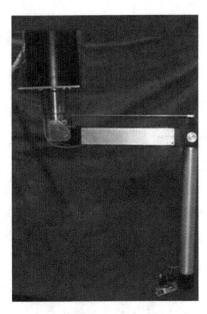

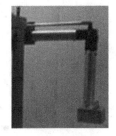

Fig. 2. Photograph of master arm

Fig. 1. Photograph of slave arm

2.1   The Slave Arm

The slave arm has five articulated joints and a gripper. All these joints have electric motors along with feedback devices. The various manipulator motions are illustrated in Fig. 3.

The general specification of CSM is given below:

- Degree of freedom: 5
- Payload: 3 kg
- Maximum Reach: 1 m
- Gripper opening: 20 mm

2.2   The Master Arm

The master arm is a scaled down version of the slave arm and provided with the necessary sensors for initialization and operation in master-slave mode. The compactness of the master arm allows it to be mounted close to the shielding window for better visibility during its operation. The various master motions are illustrated in Fig. 4.

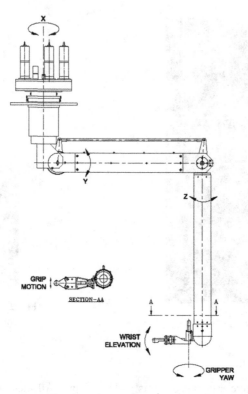

Fig. 3. Joint axes of slave arm

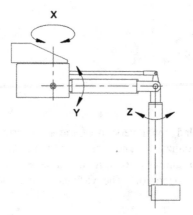

Fig. 4. Joint axes of master arm

3   Control System of CSM

The control system for the manipulator is built around position servo controller with built in PLC. The system is so designed that the control panel is compact and suited to the portable nature of the application. The system draws power from a standard single-phase AC supply through an umbilical cord, while all necessary control and drive power requirements are met through onboard converters.

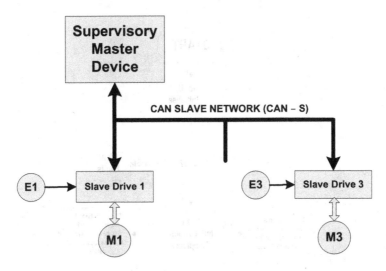

Fig. 5. Architecture of control system

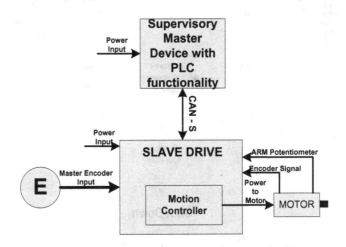

Fig. 6. Functional block diagram of drive

3.1   Control System Design and Hardware

This manipulator is based on distributed digital control, based on standard CAN Open protocol. The 5-DOF manipulator has 3 joints working in the master-slave servo mode, while the lower two joints are operated in open loop controls.

This control system consists of Supervisory servo controller, configured as a CAN Master, 3 servo drives, operating as CAN Slaves, for control of Joints 1 to 3 and the necessary HMI for the operation and parameterization of the system. The supervisory controller has in-built PLC, which monitors and controls the complete system.

The actuators use Brushed DC motors with Incremental Encoders for sensing and tracking of the rotor position. The control system provides facilities for mode selection,

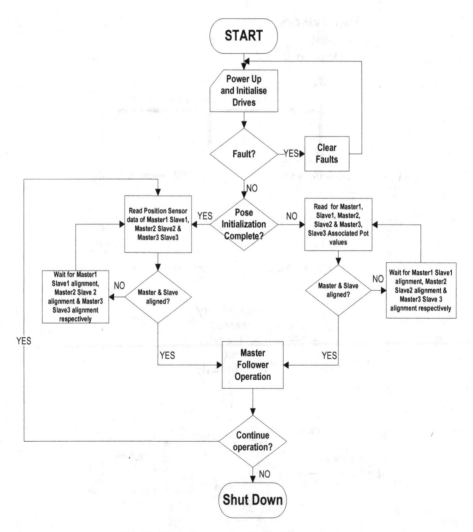

Fig. 7. Flow diagram for manipulator operation

joint speed selection for joints 4 and 5, etc. As the control processing system is distributed, it reduces individual unit processing requirements. It also supports high update rate and larger number of input-output signals required by each servo loop. Also, it is less vulnerable to total system failure. This architecture allows the necessary quick data transfer between the master supervisory device and the slave drive. The Data sampling and information transfer are accomplished in real time. Figure 5 shows the architecture of the control system and Fig. 6 shows the functional block diagram of the drive.

The supervisory controller executes an application program for controlling the system operation and command generation for slaves in the network. The controller periodically monitors the input information from the master joint sensors and then sends motion commands to the slave arm actuators, which faithfully follows the master signal to produce the master-slave joint motion. The operation of the manipulator is through a combination of closed loop servo control and open loop digital controls. The master arm is provided with a potentiometer for initial absolute position sensing. This is used for the alignment of the master and slave joints at power up. The joint potentiometers provided on each of the joints are then used for the master-slave motion. Figure 7 shows the logical flow chart for the manipulator operations.

The Fig. 8 shows the master following for one of the joints of the manipulator. It is evident that the operation of the master-slave mode is as per the requirements and the parameters of following accuracy and time lag are within acceptable limits.

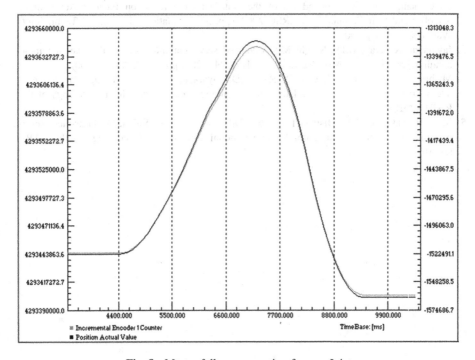

Fig. 8. Master follower operation for one Joint

4 Conclusion

The Division of Remote Handling and Robotics (DRHR) at BARC has been frontrunner for providing remote handling equipments, like master-slave manipulators, for various DAE units. However most of these equipments are designed for standardized hot-cells and thus follow the standard specifications for size, payloads and mounting arrangements. In case of remote handling requirements for radioactive facilities other than Hot-cells, special equipments are required to be developed which usually cater to a specific requirement. The Development of CSM has resulted in establishing the technology required for the design of miniature servo manipulators has been established. The CSM is so designed that it is amenable to adaption for specific application while retaining the general nature of the equipment such that it can be used for other requirements which may arise in the facility. The development of the CSM has established the technology for the design and deployment of such remote handling equipment in future with short development times.

References

1. Jayarajan, K., Singh, M.: Master-slave manipulators: technology and recent developments. BARC News Letter, Issue No. 269, pp. 2–12, June 2006
2. Sony, B., Mahadev, V., Jayarajan, K., Singh, M.: Development of sealed three piece master slave manipulator. In: Proceedings of the National Conference on Factory Automation, Robotics and Soft Computing (FARSC-2007), pp. 52–57. National Institute of Technology, Warangal, January 2007
3. Jayarajan, K., Ray, D.D., Singh, M.: Advanced servo manipulator: a milestone in remote handling technology. BARC News Letter, Issue No. 283, pp. 2–13, August 2007
4. Mishra, J.K., Rao, M.N., Biswas, D., Ray, D.D., Jayarajan, K., Singh, M.: Development of a telerobot: a master slave manipulator with autonomous capabilities. In: Proceedings of the RAPT (2010)
5. Sony, B., Sakrikar, R.V., Biswas, D.C., Ray, D.D., Jayarajan, K., Singh, M.: Four-piece servo manipulator: a servo manipulator for conventional hotcells. In: Proceedings of the RAPT (2010)

An Evolution of Remote Handling Technology for the Indian Nuclear Research and Industry Scenario

Debasish Datta Ray[✉], J.K. Mishra, R.V. Sakrikar, Surendra Singh Saini, Ushnish Sarkar, and Tumapala Teja Swaroop

Division of Remote Handling and Robotics Bhabha Atomic Research Centre, Mumbai, India
{dray,jmishra,rsakrikar,sainiss,ushinish,tejswrp}@barc.gov.in

Abstract. Remote Handling is an essential tool for radioactive material handling and nuclear fuel reprocessing. Division of Remote Handling and Robotics, Bhabha Atomic Research Centre has been working on the development of remote handling tools for in house applications. The experience in each development has germinated the development of a more advanced system. This paper tries to graph this evolution of remote handling technology as an indispensable part of the Nuclear Fuel Fabrication and Fuel Reprocessing. The paper also encompasses a moderately detailed description of the methodologies associated with the development.

Keywords: Remote handling · Master slave manipulator · Servo manipulator

1 Introduction

Remotization plays a vital role in all nuclear installations. Plants using Thorium based fuels introduce additional requirements in the U-232 decay chain. In such plants, operators can handle the material only behind thick shields, using reliable remote handling tools. In radioactive material handling, uncertainty in task definition and precise descriptions makes fixed automation difficult to apply. Hence, the majority of remote handling operations are carried out through the Master Slave manipulators. In general, a Master Slave manipulator consists of two arms – the Slave arm located in a hazardous area and the Master arm in the control station. When the operator grasps and manipulates the Master arm, the motions of his hand are reproduced at the Slave arm performing the necessary task. Division of Remote Handling and Robotics, Bhabha Atomic Research Centre has been involved in the design and development of Master Slave manipulator systems, since long. The development process has evolved with time circumscribing change and advancement ranging from basic technology paradigm to more detailed and involved control engineering features and methodologies. A streamlined overview of this evolution will be presented in subsequent sections. The description of the evolution process, for ease of tracking, will be decoupled into evolution of basic approach to remotization and evolution of controls.

© Springer Nature Singapore Pte Ltd. 2016
B. Vinod et al. (Eds.): ICAARS 2016, CCIS 627, pp. 11–20, 2016.
DOI: 10.1007/978-981-10-2845-8_2

2 Evolution from Mechanical Master Slave Manipulator to Electrical Servo Manipulator

The venture started with the construction of Mechanical Master Slave Manipulator [1, 2]. The mechanical manipulators are most generally through-the-wall-type, where a through-tube passing through a shield wall between the operator and hot cell connects the Master and Slave mechanisms. The basic layout is shown in Fig. 1.

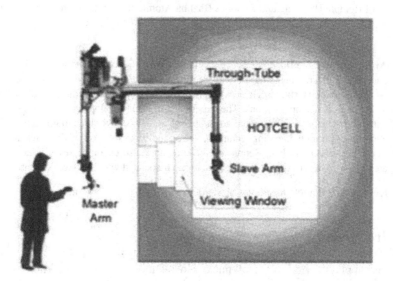

Fig. 1. Basic layout of mechanical master slave manipulators in hot-cell

There are mainly two types of mechanical manipulator designs: telescopic (Fig. 2) and articulated (Fig. 3). The fundamental difference between the two is that in an articulated manipulator all the joints are revolute while in a telescopic manipulator, one or more joints may be prismatic. Typically, each arm is a 6 degree of freedom serial mechanism. The mechanical coupling between the Master and the Slave arm is designed to be bilateral such that the forces acting at the Slave arm are reflected back to the Master arm in order to render the operator a real feel of the remote environment.

The mechanical coupling between the Master and Slave manipulator evidently limits the degree of remotization. The slave arm has to be fixed at one point only, in the hot-cell. Force reflection from Slave arm to Master arm, being unchangeable, often fatigues the operator after prolonged operations. All these practical problems led to the development of Electrical Servo Manipulators.

In Electrical Servo Manipulators, the Slave arm and the Master arm are coupled electrically/electronically and no mechanical coupling between them is present. The slave arm is actuated by motors. The controller, continuously monitors joint angles of Master and Slave arms using sensors like potentiometer and resolver, and drives the Slave motor appropriately to correct any deviation in angle between corresponding joints of Master and Slave. Force reflection, at Master, rendered by mirroring Slave motor

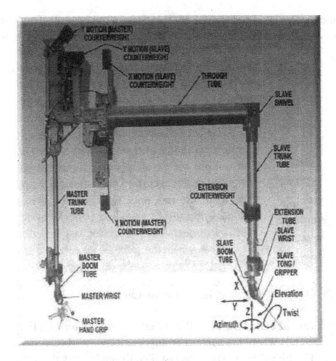

Fig. 2. Telescopic manipulator

Fig. 3. Articulated manipulator

current on the corresponding Master motor, can be scaled through a program thereby offering the operator the opportunity to work at his/her comfort level without fatigue. The slave arm now does not have to be fixed to the master arm physically, and a transporter can be used to move the Slave arm required to approach hot-cell equipment from different positions and directions, providing flexibility in equipment layout in the hot-cell. The effective range of the Slave arm thereby increases manifolds, and even a single pair of Slave arms can serve a large cell. The task area is viewed using CCTV cameras mounted on the manipulator and at different locations in the hot-cell. This generation of manipulators are called the Advanced Servo Manipulators (ASM) [3] (Fig. 4).

Fig. 4. Advanced servo manipulator

A particular variant called the Four Piece Servo Manipulator [4] (FPSM) has been developed for hot-cells where the support arrangement for ASM (e.g. transporters etc.) is not available. The FPSM (Fig. 5) can be installed through the wall sleeves of existing hot-cells.

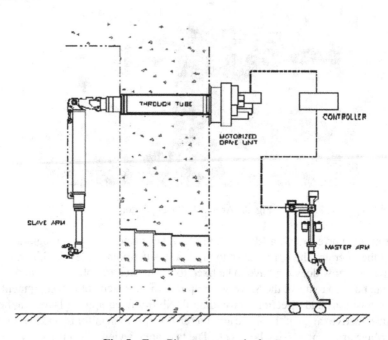

Fig. 5. Four Piece servo manipulator

Once the remote handling technology has undergone a paradigm shift from Mechanical Master Slave Manipulator to Electrical Servo Manipulators, further development has been generational, bringing in improvement in the control architecture and functional features in both hardware and software. This will be discussed in the next section.

3   Evolution of the Electrical Servo Manipulator Control Architecture and Features

The Advanced Servo Manipulator (ASM), till now, has 2 generations of development which are discussed in subsequent subsections.

3.1   ASM Gen I

The control architecture of the first generation of the Advanced Servo Manipulator (ASM GEN I) is shown in Fig. 6. It is a multi-axis bidirectional tightly coupled digital distributed control system. The main components of the Servo Control System are the actuator, the drive, the joint controller, the Master computer and the communication pathway that connects them all. All the ASM developments use Brushless AC Servo motors with inbuilt failsafe brakes and Resolver as the actuators. The control of these actuators and hence the entire manipulator control is centred on indigenously developed BLAC Servo motor drives. The functional block diagram of the motor drive is shown in Fig. 7. The position control is based on PI control (Fig. 8). It is cascade control architecture as evident. The Speed PI control and Torque PI control is built into the Servo Control IC, while the Position PI control is implemented in the Joint Controller, which in turn communicates with the Master Control PC.

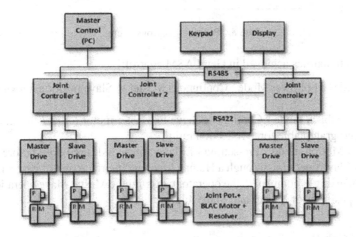

Fig. 6. Control architecture of Gen I Advanced servo manipulator

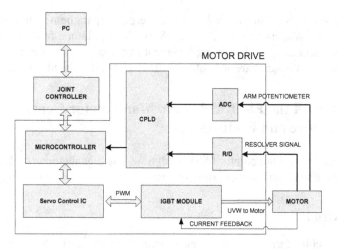

Fig. 7. Functional block diagram of motor drive

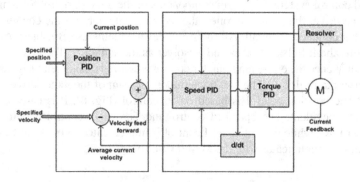

Fig. 8. Position Control system

The functionalities achieved in Gen I ASM control:

1. Master Slave Follower Mode - Continuous Master to Slave position tracking for all joints
2. Force Feedback mode - Continuous Slave to Master motor torque/current tracking with a programmable force reflection ratio
3. Indexed Motion mode - Pre-setting of Slave arm to a desired pose before starting Master Slave operation through a Human Machine Interface (in this case a keypad). After indexing is completed, the operator can continue Master Slave operation from the set positions of Master and Slave joints.

3.2   ASM Gen II

The 2nd Generation of ASM opened up a wide range of opportunities for the technology. This has been made possible by a change in the control architecture [5] (Fig. 9).

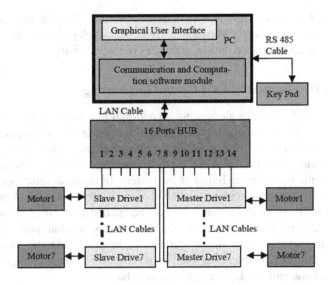

Fig. 9. Control architecture of Gen II Advanced servo manipulator

In Gen I control architecture the Joint Controller is microcontroller based embedded system with limited computation power. In Gen II, coordinating computer has become major control loop executive, thereby increasing the flexibility of implementing computation intensive features for intelligent and seamless human-robot-environment interface. In addition to the already existing features from Gen I, the functionalities achieved in Gen II ASM are:

(1) Robot Mode - The slave arm can be controlled directly from the coordinating PC without using the Master arm either in Joint space or in world coordinates. The control software also provides features for programming motion sequence scripts for the Slave arm. Apart from the Manipulator end effector position, the manipulating forces exerted by the end effector can also be simultaneously controlled [6].

(2) Teach-n-Playback Mode - In case of a repetitive job in an episodic environment (e.g. pick up some object from a predefined place and placing it at some other predefined place), the operator can teach the Slave arm the required sequence of motions, which will be recorded in the system and later played back by the Slave arm. The playback speed can be varied and the playback sequence can be totally reversed also.

(3) Constrained Motion and Obstacle Avoidance - This feature through artificial forces at the Master arm guide the operator to maintain motion along predefined workspace constraints (e.g. when manipulating objects in a cylindrical pipe, the preferential direction of motion is the cylinder axis; when performing welding on a surface, preferential motion should be confined to the plane of welding) while avoiding predefined workspace obstacles which the manipulator should not hit [7].

Besides these, methodologies like friction compensation [8] for faithful and accurate force reflection from Slave to the Master arm, have been developed which have enhanced system performance and added to the capabilities of the technology.

3.3   Further Development in ASM Control Engineering

Till Generation II, for Joint angle sensing, in addition to Resolvers, absolute position feedback devices like potentiometer was required for power-up initialization, because the Resolvers, although accurate and reliable otherwise, cannot provide the last joint position at system power-up. Every extra electro-mechanical component like potentiometer adds to the maintenance issues of the system. In recent development of a new version of Servo drive, an onboard NVRAM periodically stores the data from the Resolver so that the last known actuator state can be fetched during the next power cycle for initialization. This feature eliminates the need of any absolute position feedback device. Also, in the earlier system, configuration of the drive had to be done through a specific JTAG interface. In the newer version of the drive, all these configurations can be done through the uniform LAN communication backbone.

3.4   Performance Evaluation

Although performance evaluation of the system is not directly the focus of this paper, for the sake of completion, the most fundamental capabilities of ASM namely Master Slave Follower and Force Reflection have been evaluated and graphically illustrated. A detailed coverage of all the other features can be found in [5–8]. In Fig. 10, the overlapping of the motion profiles of the Master and Slave joint indicate proper Master following of the Slave. In Fig. 11, the reflected Master torque profile is same as that of

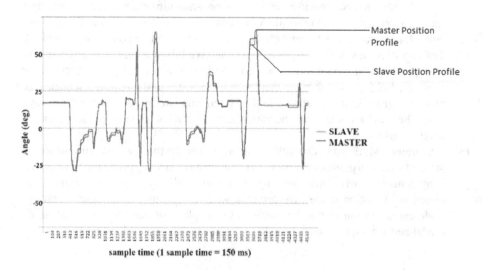

Fig. 10. Master to slave position tracking

the Slave torque profile, only scaled down and spurious noises smoothened down for operator ease.

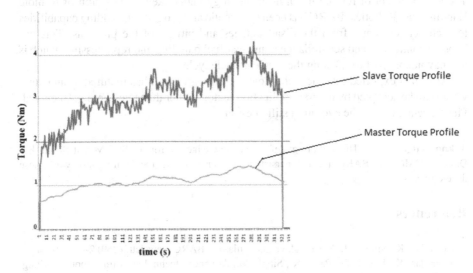

Fig. 11. Slave torque and reflected master torque

The accuracy and repeatability of the ASM Gen II in Robot Mode has been evaluated according to ISO 9283 [9]. They were found to be respectively 27.74 mm and 8.74 mm respectively.

4   Application of Master Slave Manipulator Technology

Mechanical Master Slave manipulator, since long time have found wide application in hot-cells across different facilities of the Department of Atomic Energy, Govt. of India. A master slave manipulator pair and other accessories were supplied to INS Tunir, Uran, for remote missile fuelling. Gen II ASM is now ready to be installed at Waste Immobilisation Plant, Bhabha Atomic Research Centre. One variant of FPSM is going to be installed at Tarapur Atomic Power Station for Reactor maintenance jobs.

5   Future Developments

The success obtained in the present developments has motivated us to delve into newer avenues. The foremost of them, which in future, may form the Generation III of Servo manipulator technology is the introduction of a wearable exoskeleton as the Master device and its subsequent interfacing with the Slave manipulator. Such systems will not only be more user friendly, but will also be able to provide richer haptic (force feedback) experiences. Robot assisted surgery is another futuristic technology for which we are developing reliable and accurate miniature master slave manipulator systems.

6 Conclusion

The advancement of remote handling technology undertaken by Division of Remote Handling and Robotics, BARC has been systematic and progressive, adding capabilities to each version learnt from the disadvantages and pitfalls of the previous. This has boosted confidence and self-reliance in nuclear fuel handling and reprocessing which is an unavoidable part for closing the Nuclear Fuel Cycle.

Also, it is expected that the technology, still progressing, has matured to an extent which can be accepted by diverse application sectors, other than nuclear, e.g. Chemical, Pharmaceutical etc. The evolution still goes on.

Acknowledgements. The authors gratefully acknowledge the role of Shri Manjit Singh, Ex. Director DM&AG, BARC for his persistent guidance during the entire journey of these developments.

References

1. Jayarajan, K., Singh, M.: Master slave manipulators. BARC Newslett. (269) 2–12 (2006)
2. Jayarajan, K., Ray, D.D., Pal, P.K., Singh, M.: Advanced technologies for remote handling. In: Proceedings of the International Conference on Peaceful Uses of Atomic Energy, pp. 645–646 (2009)
3. Jayarajan, K., Mishra, J.K., Ray, D.D., Rao, M.N., Biswas, D., Singh, M.: Development of advanced servo manipulator for remote handling in nuclear installations. In: Proceedings of the National Conference on Robotics and Intelligent Manufacturing Process (RIMP-2009) (2009)
4. Sakrikar, R.V., Sarkar, U., Ray, D.D., Biswas, D.C., Jayarajan, K.: Development of prototype four piece servo manipulator: a novel remote handling technology for nuclear facilities. In: Proceedings of 1st International Conference on Advances in Robotics, New York, NY, USA. ACM (2013). doi:10.1145/2506095.2506152
5. Ray, D.D., Singh, M.: Development of a force reflecting tele-robot for remote handling in nuclear installations. In: Proceedings of the 21st International Conference on Applied Robotics for the Power Industry (2010). doi:10.1109/CARPI.2010.5624456
6. Tumapala, T., Saini, S.S., Sarkar, U., Ray, D.D.: Compliance control of tele – Robot. In: Proceedings of Conference on Advances In Robotics (AIR 2013), New York, NY, USA. ACM (2013). Article 33. doi:10.1145/2506095.2506114
7. Sarkar, U., Saini, S.S., Ray, D.D.: Constrained motion and obstacle avoidance based on assistive forces for tele-operation in hot-cells. In: Proceedings of Conference on Advances in Robotics (AIR 2013), New York, NY, USA. ACM (2013). Article 44. doi: 10.1145/2506095.2506139
8. Saini, S.S., Sarkar, U., Ray, D.D.: Friction compensation for sensor-less force reflection in servo manipulators for high radiation areas. In: Proceedings of Conference on Advances in Robotics (AIR 2013), New York, NY, USA. ACM (2013). Article 44. doi: 10.1145/2506095.2506139
9. ISO 9283 Second Edition 1998-04-01, "Manipulating Industrial Robots- performance criteria and related test methods"

Industrial Robotics

Rigid Body Transformations for Calibration of Prototype Fast Breeder Reactor, Steam Generator Inspection Device

S. Joseph Winston[1(✉)], Joel Jose[1], Arun Subramaniyan[2],
S. Murugan[1], and A.K. Bhaduri[1]

[1] Indira Gandhi Centre for Atomic Research, Kalpakkam, India
{winston,joel,murugan,bhaduri}@igcar.gov.in
[2] Electrical and Electronics Department, BITS Pilani, Pilani, India
sarun2006klin@gmail.com

Abstract. Prototype Fast Breeder Reactor (PFBR) has 8 Steam Generators (SG), each with 547 tubes connecting top and bottom headers. Sodium flows in the shell side and the water/steam in the tube side. The integrity of these tubes is ascertained by periodic in-service inspection (ISI) procedures. Remote Field Eddy Current Testing (RFEC) is preferred as the SG tubes are ferromagnetic. Inverse kinematic (IK) algorithm has been developed and implemented in the motion controller for two axis system. The precise reach of tubes is often limited due to errors introduced during deployment. This paper details the use of the joint axis motor encoders to compute the error vectors through a simple forward kinematics. Singular Value Decomposition (SVD) of the correlation matrix obtained from the transformed points reveal the Euler rotation matrix which is the error rotation of the device and subsequently the translation error matrix is deduced. The sensitivity study on calibration is also carried out by inducing errors in the vertical axis error measurement. This paper details the SG inspection device calibration method which reduces cost, time and effort for the inspection.

Keywords: Steam generator · Inspection system · Calibration · Robot · Correlation matrix · Singular value decomposition(SVD) · Error correction · Error sensitivity · Damped least squares (DLS) · Inverse kinematics

1   Introduction

Prototype Fast Breeder reactor (PFBR), Steam generators (SG) are 8 in numbers and have sodium in the primary shell side and water/steam in the secondary tube side. SG is about 23 m height. Figure 1 shows a typical SG. Periodic inspection of the tubes enhances the safety and also significantly reduces the operational cost through life extensions. Vision and remote Field Eddy Current Testing (RFEC) is generally carried out to qualify the tubes which separates sodium and water. Around the world SG inspection is more challenging and involves complex devices to enter and carryout the tube inspection [1]. The accessibility to the entire axial length of the tubes is only possible from the top header manhole. The inspection device has a deployment module

© Springer Nature Singapore Pte Ltd. 2016
B. Vinod et al. (Eds.): ICAARS 2016, CCIS 627, pp. 23–40, 2016.
DOI: 10.1007/978-981-10-2845-8_3

to lower the 2-axis robotic arm to reach closer to the tube sheet where all the tubes end at the SG top header. The two axis arm work plane is referenced to the tube sheet plane, only through long mechanical structural route which includes the mechanical assembly of the device, manhole flange, top header and the tube sheet unlike the conventional robots have a well reference fixed rigid bases. The accuracy of the inspection device depends on orientation of the deployed inspection device and also fabrication accuracies. Since the SG structure and the inspection device structures are considered to be rigid bodies, it is quite encouraging to understand that the inspection device will have a work plane and the tube sheet another. Once the inspection device is placed on the manhole for the inspection, the challenge is to remotely relate the coordinate center of the inspection device to the coordinate center of the tube sheet. This paper deals with the novel idea to use the motor encoders used for the shoulder and elbow arm

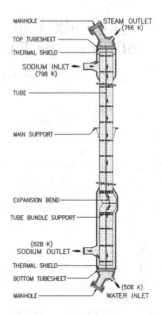

Fig. 1. Steam generator

actuation of the 2 axis system robotic arm to measure the error through a forward kinematic transform at difference tube sheet known locations and perform the Singular Value decomposition of the correlation matrix obtained from the measured to the actual theoretical values. By rigid body transformation, the rotation and the translation matrices are obtained which will be used for the correction on the fly, to reach each of the 547 tubes in the tube sheet through the Damped Least squares inverse kinematics, programmed in the motion controller. The Damped Least Squares Inverse Kinematic algorithm is implemented on the GMAS ELMO motion controller. Numerical implementation of SVD to compute the error Rotation matrix from the correlation matrix is quite expensive through a motion controller which is basically dedicated to control the axis motors. Hence, the encoder data from the controller is sent through a TCP/IP socket. Raspberry pi module receives the data and the rigid body transformation matrix is computed through the developed python code for SVD. The error Transformation matrix computed is then forwarded to the GMAS controller. In order to reach the tubes with error coordinates, the actual coordinate values are transformed through this transformation matrix and for this transformed points, the inverse kinematics is carried out to obtain the joint space variables to reach the tubes accurately. The entire process is done without reorienting the device and hence reduces significant cost, time and effort.

2   PFBR SG Inspection System-PSGIS

The complete inspection device, PSGIS has several modules performing various tasks as that of Inspection cable handling, device deployment, tube locating module, cable pushing module, Inspection system module etc. It is required to uniquely identify all the tubes and designate them with tube numbers to reference the tube inspection data against each tubes. The Tube Locator Module is a two axis robotic arm which orients to all 547 tubes of SG for pushing the RFEC probe or visual probe for inspection.

3   Tube Locator Module-TLM

The geometrical shape of TLM is designed to have the arm fit inside the deployment module which is placed into the manhole at the top header of the SG from where the system is deployed into the header. Figure 2 shows the TLM. Since the tube sheet is planar, selective compliant arm is designed and used. The kinematic move of the shoulder and elbow axes will make the end effecter i.e. the cable pushing module to orient to the tubes in the tube sheet plane. The tube number to the Cartesian coordinates with reference to the coordinate frame of the tube sheet and the inverse kinematic algorithm developed and implemented on the motion controller.

Fig. 2. Tube locator module

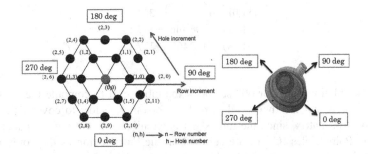

Fig. 3. Tube ordering scheme to reduce lookup table

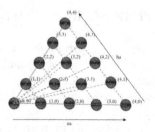

Fig. 4. Dummy tube sheet & tube/hole numbering

3.1   Tube Sheet and Calibration Point Tubes/Holes- CPH

The tubes connecting the bottom header and the top header end in the tube sheet. They are in hexagonal pattern increasing in row from 0 to 14. The row 0 represents the center tube. The hole/tube number starts from 0 and runs through the hexagonal pattern as shown in Fig. 3. Figure 4 shows a dummy tube sheet and the tube ordering scheme for one small sector. Thus the tube center can be referenced from the center of the tube sheet in polar coordinate frame as shown in Eq. 1. Accordingly the tube center Cartesian coordinate is obtained from Eq. 2. This representation eliminates the storing up of all 547 tubes coordinate data in the form of lookup table into the small memory available in the motion controller. Hence, from the user input row number and tube/hole number the tube center coordinate values are computed before the IK algorithm is used to compute joint space angles for running the motors.

$$(r, \theta) = \left(a\sqrt{n^2 + h^2 - nh}, \cos^{-1}\left(\frac{a(2n - h)}{2r}\right)\right) \tag{1}$$

$$\begin{bmatrix} x \\ y \end{bmatrix} = \begin{pmatrix} r\cos\theta \\ r\sin\theta \end{pmatrix} \tag{2}$$

a -Tube pitch, 32.2 mm

Table 1. Calibration point tubes/holes

Tube	X	Y
(11,0)	0	354.2
(11,22)	−306.746	−177.1
(11,44)	306.746	−177.1

This formulation done for 60° sector of the tube sheet to compute the coordinate values of tube center are then used to deduce for other sectors to cover all 360° by using a rotation matrix, since the tube sheet is circular symmetric in the pattern. The Calibration Point Holes (CPH), are selected on the outer region as they only can be easily identified from the actual tube sheet tube pattern. The vision camera at the end of the elbow arm is used to locate the tubes from the tube array pattern remotely. Tube order scheme is followed to compute the coordinate values of all the 547 tubes by referring to the row number and the tube number. Table 1 shows the Calibration Point Holes and their respective coordinate values. Figure 5 shows the CPH.

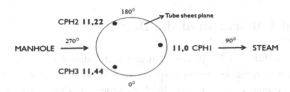

Fig. 5. Calibration point holes/tubes

3.2 Damped Least Squares (DLS) Inverse Kinematics for TLM

The joint space variables are related to the end effecter Cartesian space coordinates through the Jacobian matrix. Generally when the Jacobian matrix is a non square matrix, a pseudo inverse is carried out to perform the inversion of the Jacobian.

The forward kinematics shows the end effecter a function of joint space variables and shown in Eq. 3;

$$[e] = J[\theta] \tag{3}$$

Inverse Kinematic equation is as in Eq. 4;

$$[\theta] = J^{-1}[e] \tag{4}$$

$$J = \frac{df}{dx} = \begin{bmatrix} \frac{\partial f}{\partial x_1} \cdots \frac{\partial f}{\partial x_n} \end{bmatrix} = \begin{bmatrix} \frac{\partial f1}{\partial x1} & \cdots & \frac{\partial f1}{\partial xn} \\ \vdots & \ddots & \vdots \\ \frac{\partial fm}{\partial x1} & \cdots & \frac{\partial fm}{\partial xn} \end{bmatrix} \tag{5}$$

The Jacobian matrix is shown in Eq. 5. The pseudo inverse is named after Moore-Penrose. In all practical cases, considering the arm stability close to the singular position, the Damped Least squares (DLS) Inverse [2] is used which is shown in Eq. 6.

$$J^+ = J^T(JJ^T + \lambda^2 I)^{-1} \tag{6}$$

Where λ *is a damping factor.*

When the value of $\lambda = 0$, the Eq. 6 inverse will work typically as a pseudo inverse. Further, though this λ strengthens the diagonal elements of Jacobian near singular positions, it causes some errors in the end effecter tracing path which is insignificant. However this has no effect on the position reach of the TLM and is neglected.

Since the computation of the joint space variables from the Cartesian space is non-linear and the Jacobian is dependent on the pose/orientation of the TLM arm, the solution has to be on an iterative basis in discrete steps. The two axis inverse kinematic solver has been written in python scripting for the simulation purpose and targeted on the motion controller through the programming standard IEC 61131-3 User Function Block Diagrams (UFBD) created out of Structured Text (ST) code similar to a C language syntax.

4   Errors and Calibration of the Device

The tube locator module (TLM) device is inserted through the manhole at an angle of 60° by a deployment module during inspection. The tube sheet has to be referenced from the manhole flange surface where the deployment module is mounted. The errors in the mounting of the inspection device causes a change in the orientation of the TLM with respect to the tube sheet plane. This significantly affects the performance of the device thereby missing the target tube for inspection while reaching through the Inverse Kinematics on the arm. These errors as such are not measurable through external sources as the access into the man hole is limited to the device only. Hence the exploitation of the motor encoders which are generally present in any robotic 2 axis systems to easily carry out without any additional sensor devices.

4.1   Possible Errors

The culmination of errors from the fabrication as well as mounting of the device can result in the form of combined rotation as well as translation errors. They can be well addressed as a coordinate system transformation from tube sheet plane to the device working plane.

Rotation Error. Error in mounting the device which is due to circular symmetry and may have rotation on the axis of the deployment module along the manhole or may be caused due to fabrication tolerances causing a twist of the device. Figure 6 shows the rotation error in the device.

Fig. 6. Rotation error

Translation Error. Error due to device deployment module extending the deployment or falling short of the target position along with errors due to fabrication tolerances. This generates translations errors. Figure 7 shows the translation error.

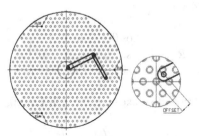

Fig. 7. Translation error

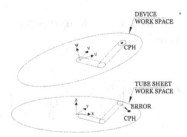

Fig. 8. Coordinate frame

4.2   Errors Represented as 3-D Right Body Transformations

The deployment module error manifests into 3 orthogonal rotations. The combined rotation cannot be decomposed to individual rotation as the matrix multiplications are noncommutative. Figure 8 shows the tube sheet and the device work plane coordinate system. It is desired to use only the Euler rotation and use the rotation elements on the combined rotation matrix for the error correction. If the θ_1, θ_2 and θ_3 are angles that represent the rotation on the axes X, Y and Z, the rotation matrices are shown as 3×3 matrix and the combined transformation matrix incorporating rotation and translation are represented as a 4×4 matrix.

Rotation error about X axis

$$R_x = \begin{pmatrix} 1 & 0 & 0 \\ 0 & \cos\theta_1 & \sin\theta_1 \\ 0 & -\sin\theta_1 & \cos\theta_1 \end{pmatrix} \qquad (7)$$

Rotation error about Y axis

$$R_y = \begin{pmatrix} \cos\theta_2 & 0 & \sin\theta_2 \\ 0 & 1 & 0 \\ -\sin\theta_2 & 0 & \cos\theta_2 \end{pmatrix} \tag{8}$$

Rotation error about Z axis

$$R_z = \begin{pmatrix} \cos\theta_3 & \sin\theta_3 & 0 \\ -\sin\theta_3 & \cos\theta_3 & 0 \\ 0 & 0 & 1 \end{pmatrix} \tag{9}$$

Translation error in 3 respective axes are show in Eq. 10;

$$T = \begin{pmatrix} x_0 \\ y_0 \\ z_0 \end{pmatrix} \tag{10}$$

Combined Transformation matrix which incorporates rotation and translation together in a 4 × 4 matrix is as in Eq. 11;

$$M = TR = \begin{pmatrix} r_{11} & r_{12} & r_{13} & x_0 \\ r_{21} & r_{22} & r_{23} & y_0 \\ r_{31} & r_{32} & r_{33} & z_0 \\ 0 & 0 & 0 & 1 \end{pmatrix} \tag{11}$$

4.3   Calculating the Error Transformation Matrix

The shoulder and elbow arm of TLM by virtue of interconnected rigid bodies will trace all the coordinates in its work space which is a plane. Hence tube sheet coordinate points always will get transformed respecting the rigid body transformation. Converse to the transformation of a set of tube sheet points to device work space points by transformation matrix; one has to deduce the transformation matrix from the actual tube sheet points to the device work space points considering the rigid body transformation. Hence in the present work a few selected points 3 or more which are easily identifiable from the tube sheet through vision sensors have been used to compute the actual transformation that exists between the coordinate center of tube sheet and device work plane. This transformation matrix will be used to transform all the 547 tube sheet holes to be mapped to the device coordinate frame.

Let us assume the set of coordinate points from the tube sheet, selected for the calibration be {mi}. The transformed set of {mi} points is denoted as {di} which is after the error measurement. R and T are the rotation and translation matrices that transformed {mi} points to {di}. Solving the optimal transformation that maps the set {mi} onto {di} requires minimizing a least squares error criterion [3] given by

$$\Sigma^2 = \sum_{i=1}^{N} \|di - Rmi - T\|^2 \tag{12}$$

$$\bar{d} = \frac{1}{N} \sum_{i=1}^{N} di \tag{13}$$

$$d_{ci} = d_i - \bar{d} \tag{14}$$

$$\bar{m} = \frac{1}{N} \sum_{i=1}^{N} mi \tag{15}$$

$$m_{ci} = m_i - \bar{m} \tag{16}$$

Equation 12 can be rewritten as:

$$\Sigma^2 = \sum_{i=1}^{N} \left(d_{ci}^T d_{ci} + m_{ci}^T m_{ci} - 2d_{ci}^T R m_{ci} \right) \tag{17}$$

This equation is minimized when the term $2d_{ci}^T R m_{ci}$ is maximized which is equivalent to maximizing Trace (RH), where H is a correlation matrix which is defined by;

$$H = \sum_{i=1}^{N} m_{ci} d_{ci}^T \tag{18}$$

If the singular value decomposition of H is given by $H = U \Sigma V^T$, then the optimal rotation matrix, R that maximizes the desired trace [4] is;

$$R = VU^T \tag{19}$$

In order to correct the rotation matrix on some case which represents reflection rather than rotation as suggested by Umeya [5] and Kanatani [6], the rotation may be computed as;

$$R = U \begin{pmatrix} 1 & 0 & 0 \\ 0 & 1 & 0 \\ 0 & 0 & \det(UV^T) \end{pmatrix} V^T \tag{20}$$

The optimal translation can be now deduced as follows;

$$T = \bar{d} - R\bar{m} \tag{21}$$

Combined error transformation matrix will be now used to transform all 547 tube center in the tube sheet before running the inverse kinematic algorithm to reach tube centers.

$$M = TR \tag{22}$$

The transformation matrix as in Eq. 22 corrects the error for the entire tube sheet for precise reach.

4.4 Error Correction Abstraction

Flow chart shown in Fig. 9 explains the procedure for the calibration.

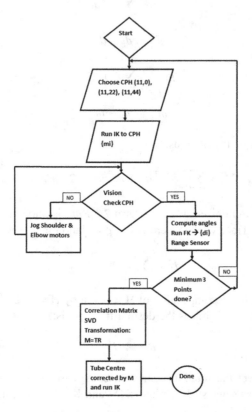

Fig. 9. Calibration abstraction

5 Results and Discussion

The calibration methodology is simulated through a PC system by Python programming before deploying into the actual inspection device. It is to be noted that the encoders used in the arm actuators are in the order of 4 lakh counts per revolution and the position accuracy gives relatively very high order of error measurements through encoders. However if there is any error in the analog range sensor, then that induces calibration errors and hence a sensitivity study also performed to see the effect of this on calibration.

5.1   Simulated Results

To check the formulated algorithm, known angles were chosen as errors i.e. $\theta_1 = 2°$, $\theta_2 = 5°$ and $\theta_3 = 10°$ and translation errors, $(x_0, y_0, z_0) = (1,1,5)$. Figure 10 shows the schematic.

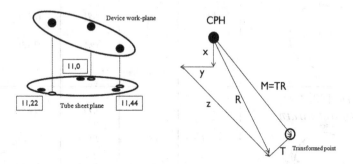

Fig. 10. Simulated error in Tube sheet and device planes

The tubes (11,0), (11,22) and (11,44) coordinate points $\{mi\}$ are transformed using the transformation matrix shown in Eqs. 7, 8, 9 and the final transformed points are taken as $\{di\}$. From the original points $\{mi\}$ and the transformed points $\{di\}$, the transformation matrix is computed through the rotation and translation as shown in Eqs. 20 and 21. This is compared with the same order of multiplying the 3 rotations and 3 translations. This gives the confidence on the rigid body transformation through the $\{mi\}$ and $\{di\}$ sets to establish the transformation matrix (Fig. 11).

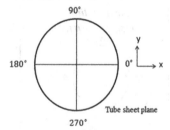

Fig. 11. Tube sheet layout

5.2   Sensitivity Analysis

Intuitively as three points are needed to fully describe a plane in $\mathbb{R}^3$, the minimum number of points needed for calibration is three. In this section, the optimum location of the three calibration points is identified. Even in the absence of mounting/fabrication errors, inaccurate measurements of the z co-ordinate of the transformed point lead to different magnitudes of error for different tubes based on the choice of number and configuration of calibration points. The motor encoder used in the TLM is devoid of backlash and hence the Cartesian co-ordinates in tube sheet plane can be measured accurately through a forward kinematic procedure using the joint space angular positions.

Table 2. Point pivoting

Location	Tube	% Error	Error mm	Max. Error Tube
a) Near center (1,0), (1,2), (1,4) 90° / 180° / 0° / 270°	(1,0)	5	0.21	(13,2)
		15	1.91	(13,2)
		50	19.82	(13,2)
b) On 180° line (10,15), (11,16), (11,17) 90° / 180° / 0° / 270°	(10,15)	5	1.14	(14,61)
		15	10.09	(14,61)
		50	92.15	(14,61)
c) Near 0° line (10,45), (11,49), (11,50) 90° / 180° / 0° / 270°	(10,45)	5	1.14	(14,19)
		15	10.09	(14,19)
		50	92.15	(14,19)
d) Near 90° line (11,0), (11,1), (11,65) 90° / 180° / 0° / 270°	(11,0)	5	3.62	(13,37)
		15	30.78	(13,37)
		50	213.77	(13,37)
e) Near 270° line (11,32), (11,33), (11,34) 90° / 180° / 0° / 270°	(11,33)	5	3.62	(13,2)
		15	30.78	(13,2)
		50	213.77	(13,2)

Table 3. Line Pivoting

Location	Tube	% Error	Error mm	Max. Error Tube
a) Vertical line (2,3), (11,0), (11,33)	(2,3)	5	0.17	(14,61)
		15	1.52	(14,62)
		50	16.04	(14,65)
b) Horizontal line (1,0), (10,15), (10, 45)	(1,0)	5	0.49	(13,37)
		15	4.39	(13,37)
		50	41.92	(13,37)
c) Diagonal line (1,5), (9,6), (9,33)	(1,5)	5	0.51	(14,33)
		15	4.59	(14,33)
		50	43.61	(14,33)

In the simulation, it is chosen a reasonable error in the z axis measurement. When the z-axis corresponding to all the three calibration points have the same error in measurement, the device work-plane is simply translated in the z-direction by the same amount and the choice of calibration points has no effect. The worst case arises when a single calibration point is incorrectly measured (or has a different error magnitude compared to the other two points).

It is found that when the three points are arranged so as to resemble an equilateral triangle of maximum area, the sensitivity of the error is minimum. An alternative to the optimum configuration is choosing a cluster of nearby tubes 6 to 12 numbers on the tube sheet plane for calibration. Table 2 shows the set of points selected close to each other in different locations, near center and at other angular directions.

The tube sheet tube pitch is 32.2 mm and hence errors are simulated as a percentage of this. Table 2 shows that 5 %, 15 % and 50 % errors are applied on tube (1,0) and

Table 4. More points chosen for calibration

No. of tubes	Location	Tube	% Error	Error mm	Max. Tube Error
6	**Near the centre** (1,0), (1,1), (1,2), (1,3), (1,4), (1,5)		5	0.0537	(13,2)
		(1,0)	15	0.4821	(13,2)
			50	5.2574	(13,2)
9	**Near the centre** (1,0), (1,1), (1,2), (1,3), (1,4), (1,5), (2,0), (2,3), (2,6)		5	0.0047	(14,78)
		(1,0)	15	0.0422	(14,78)
			50	0.4685	(14,78)
12	**Near the centre** (1,0), (1,1), (1,2), (1,3), (1,4), (1,5), (2,0), (2,2), (2,3), (2,4), (2,5), (2,6)	(1,0)	5	0.00393	(14,75)
			15	0.0354	(14,75)
			50	0.3929	(14,75)

this yields a maximum error at tube location (13,2) such as 19.8 mm for 50 % z axis measurement. Similarly at other locations clustered points give more errors as seen in the same table.

If the selected calibration points are close to one another, a sort of point pivoting takes place which shows error magnification proportional to the radial distance of other tubes from the clustered calibration point tubes.

Table 3 shows a line pivoting when the calibration points are so chosen along a straight line or close to a straight line. The vertical line pivots, horizontal line pivots and the pivotal line where the calibration points are chosen clearly indicate the

Table 5. Optimal selection of calibration point tubes

Location	Tube	% Error	Error mm	Max. error Tube
Equilateral triangle				
(11,0), (11,22), (11,44)		5	0.002	(13,2)
[diagram of circle with triangle, 90°, 0°, 180°, 270°]	(11,0)	15	0.016	(13,2)
		50	0.177	(13,2)

calibration errors are magnified normal to the distance from the line as seen from Fig. 12 which shows the error vector.

Table 4. shows the calibration errors when more number of calibration points are chosen. The case study was done for 6, 9 and 12 number of calibration points chosen and an error of 5 %, 15 % and 50 % applied to a particular tube on the z axis. Significant reduction in the calibration error noticed when more calibration points are chosen (Fig. 13).

When the points chosen for calibration are widely spread apart, typically forming an equilateral triangle, then even with less number of calibration points (i.e. with the minimum number of points) the errors are found to be significantly reduced as seen from Table 5. This strengthens the argument of using the calibration points holes (11,0), (11,22) and (11, 44) a good choice. These tubes are also easily identifiable from the tube sheet pattern. Figure 14 shows the vector plot of the calibration error considering 3 points which form an equilateral triangle.

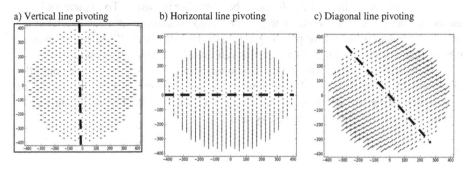

a) Vertical line pivoting   b) Horizontal line pivoting   c) Diagonal line pivoting

Fig. 12. Calibration points chosen along a line which causes line pivoting

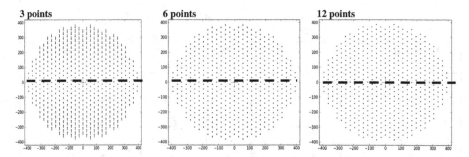

Fig. 13. More calibration points reduces error

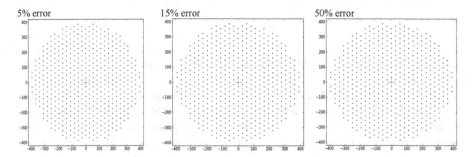

Fig. 14. Choosing widely separated calibration points reduces calibration errors

6 Implementation

It is quite expensive to implement the numerical SVD scheme into the tiny motion controllers which is already running motion controls with highest priority. Also the numerical SVD techniques are far different from the canonical way of theoretical computations of SVD [7, 8]. However an attempt was made implementing the Jacobi rotation numerical method [9] and found to be controller intensive. To implement in the inspection device, it was programmed in the motion controller to make available the axis encoder data on a TCP/IP port. Figures 15 and 16 shows the TLM and calibration mockup facility developed to ascertain the validity of the calibration parameter.

A Raspberry pi system with python is wirelessly connected to the motion controller to acquire the encoder data and populate the {di} set of points after the jogging of the motors correcting the errors manually using a vision system. Figure 17 shows the schematic layout of the implemented system.

Fig. 15. TLM on calibration table

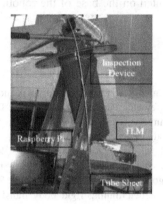

Fig. 16. Calibration setup of the complete device including TLM

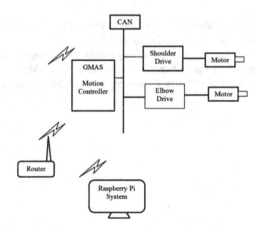

Fig. 17. Raspberry Pi module for SVD

7   Conclusion

Steam Generator inspection device requires correlating the device work and the tube sheet coordinate frame. A calibration methodology has been evolved and implemented using the SVD decomposition of the correlation matrix obtained from the theoretical tube centers to the measured deviated position of the tube center. The errors are unavoidable during the mounting of the device on the manhole for SG tube inspection and this methodology significantly reduces cost, time and effort. Also it reduces the fabrication cost by relaxing the tolerances there by correcting all the rotation and translation errors during calibration. The motor axis encoders are used to measure planar errors through forward kinematics along with the range sensor. Simulation of the rigid body transformation parameter estimation done using python scripting language. The implementation is done on the SG inspection device arm to correct the errors on the fly without re-orienting the device. This may be applicable to similar devices that need calibration when reoriented on the base of the robotic system.

References

1. Obrutsky, L., Renaud, J., Lakhan, R.: Steam generator inspections: faster, cheaper and better, are we there yet? In: IV Conferencia Panamericana de END, Buenos Aires–Octubre 2007
2. Ross, S.R.: Introduction to inverse kinematics with jacobian transpose, pseudoinverse and damped least squares method. Department of Mathematics, University of California, San Diego, 7 October 2009
3. Eggert, D.W., Lorusso, A., Fisher, R.B.: Estimating 3-D rigid body transformation: a comparison of four major algorithms. Mach. Vis. Appl. **9**(5), 272–290 (1997)
4. Challis, J.H.: A Procedure for determining rigid body transformation parameters. Biomechanics **28**, 733–737 (1995)
5. Umeyama, S.: Least Squares estimation of Transformation parameters between two point patterns. IEEE Trans. Pattern Anal. Mach. Intell. **13**, 376–380 (1991)
6. Kanatani, K.: Analysis of 3-D rotation fitting. IEEE Trans. Pattern Anal. Mach. Intell. **16**, 543–549 (1994)
7. Kalman, D.: A singular Value Decomposition: The SVD of a Matrix. The American University, Washington DC 20016, 13 February 2002
8. Wei, S., Lin, Z.: Accelerating iterations involving eigenvalue or singular value decomposition by block lanczos with warm start. Microsoft Technical Report # MSR-TR-2010–162
9. Golub, G.H., Van Loan, C.F.: Matrix Computations. The John Hopkins University Press, Baltimore (1996)

Dynamic Modelling Approaches for a 3-PPR Planar Parallel Manipulator

Vinoth Venkatesan[1], Jayant Kumar Mohanta[2],
Subir Kumar Saha[1(✉)], and Mohan Santhakumar[2]

[1] Indian Institute of Technology – Delhi, New Delhi, India
vinoth1993@gmail.com, saha@mech.iitd.ac.in
[2] Indian Institute of Technology – Indore, Indore, India
jkmjayant@gmail.com, santhakumar@iiti.ac.in

Abstract. This paper proposes two dynamic modelling approaches for a planar parallel manipulator with a 3-PPR configuration. The planar configuration has three legs each with a Prismatic-Prismatic-Revolute [PPR] configuration where the first joint is actuated. These three legs are joined by an end-effector which is in the form of an equilateral triangle. The dynamics of the manipulator was derived using an energy based Euler-Lagrangian approach and the DeNOC (Decoupled Natural Orthogonal Complement) matrices. Both the formulations are elucidated and the resulting formulation are compared under similar conditions to validate them.

Keywords: Planar parallel manipulator · Euler-Lagrangian · DeNOC matrices · Dynamics

1 Introduction

Parallel manipulators have been studied extensively in the past few decades because they are superior to the ubiquitous serial manipulators in various ways. One of the main reasons being that they can be built to be stiffer without being heavy which is because of their structure and hence they can operate at higher velocities [1]. This provides various advantages like reduced power consumption, higher kinematical precision, greater load bearing capacity, stability, higher rigidity, and suitable positional arrangement of actuators compared to serial manipulators for the same tasks.

Parallel robots have also been proven to be more precise than serial robots because they do not suffer from error accumulation. In spite of these numerous advantages, almost all of the commercial setups for providing 3-dof planar motions are based on the serial type configurations. This is mainly due to architectural complexity of the parallel manipulators and associated computations. A commercially available planar parallel manipulator is manufactured by Hephaist Seiko and is based on the 3-PRP architecture. However, the platform structure is asymmetric [2].

A lot of research has happened in the field of parallel manipulators. The forward kinematics of a wide range of manipulators have been studied by Merlet [3]. The work on the dynamics and control of parallel manipulators by Williams et al. [4] and the work on singularity analysis of planar robots stand proof to the amount of research

© Springer Nature Singapore Pte Ltd. 2016
B. Vinod et al. (Eds.): ICAARS 2016, CCIS 627, pp. 41–52, 2016.
DOI: 10.1007/978-981-10-2845-8_4

happening in this field. Despite their numerous advantages, parallel manipulators have a few limitations like the presence of complex singularities within their workspace and a limited workspace which has hindered their penetration in the commercial space as a substitute to serial manipulators [5, 6]. The study of the forward kinematic model of a class of 3-RPR configurations with the actuated joints situated in the base and their singularity analysis was done by Bonev et al. [7].

The review of literature on the present status of parallel robotic planar positioning platform has clearly shown the importance of optimum design and development in realizing a sophisticated parallel robotic $XY\theta_z$ stage and there are plenty of opportunities and lots of potentials to develop/create a better motion stage. The dynamics of these parallel manipulators can be done using several approaches. The most standard approach is the use of Euler-Lagrange approach [8]. The method is well known and documented. Apart from this, the Newton-Euler approach can be used to determine the joint torques/forces. However, this method involves the calculation of constraint forces which are not needed for controlling the platform. To overcome this, an approach based on the DeNOC matrices was proposed by Saha [9, 10] which eliminates the calculation of joint constraint forces/torques.

In this work, a 3-PPR planar parallel manipulator is presented along with its forward and inverse kinematics, and its dynamic equations of motion are derived using two different approaches. Section 2 provides the kinematics of the platform. Followed by this, Sect. 3 elucidates the Euler-Lagrange formulation. A brief of the DeNOC based formulation method using the cut-system method is provided in Sect. 4. Finally, both the formulations are compared for a specific trajectory in Sect. 5. Concluding remarks are provided in Sect. 6.

2   Kinematic Modelling

The schematic diagram of the 3-PPR manipulator is shown in Fig. 1. In can be seen that the three legs of the manipulator each have a PPR configuration with the first prismatic joint being actuated. Since the planar platform has three actuated joints, the platform has three degrees of freedom (x, y and θ_z) in the task-space of the manipulator.

The forward kinematics of the platform which represents the task-space coordinates in terms of the joint space coordinates (r_1, r_2 and r_3) – the prismatic joint coordinates of the three legs respectively – is given in (1).

$$x = r_1 - \left(\frac{r_3 - r_2}{\sqrt{3}}\right)$$

$$y = \left(\frac{r_2 + r_3}{2}\right) - \left(\frac{\sqrt{a^2 - (r_3 - r_2)^2}}{2\sqrt{3}}\right) \tag{1}$$

$$\theta_z = \sin^{-1}\left(\frac{r_3 - r_2}{a}\right)$$

where a is the side length of the end-effector which has been assumed to be an equilateral triangle. Similarly, the inverse kinematic solution of the platform which

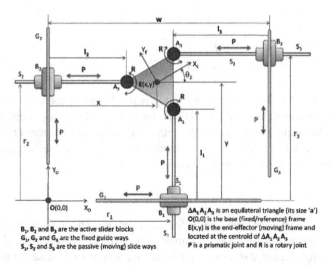

Fig. 1. The 3-PPR parallel manipulator with the kinematic parameters [11]

provides the joint-space coordinates as functions of the task-space coordinates are given by (2), i.e.,

$$r_1 = x + \left(\frac{a}{\sqrt{3}}\right)\sin(\theta_z)$$

$$r_2 = y + \left(\frac{a}{2\sqrt{3}}\right)\cos(\theta_z) - \left(\frac{a}{2}\right)\sin(\theta_z) \qquad (2)$$

$$r_3 = y + \left(\frac{a}{2\sqrt{3}}\right)\cos(\theta_z) + \left(\frac{a}{2}\right)\sin(\theta_z)$$

In order to obtain the Jacobian of the platform, we can differentiate the forward kinematic solution which will directly provide the Jacobian matrix in the form $\dot{q} = J(r)\dot{r}$, where J(r) is the Jacobian matrix, $\dot{q} = \left[\dot{x}, \dot{y}, \dot{\theta}_z\right]^T$ and $\dot{r} = [\dot{r}_1, \dot{r}_2, \dot{r}_3]^T$ are the vectors of task-space velocities and joint-space velocities, respectively.

3 Euler-Lagrangian Equations of Motion

The Euler-Lagragian equations of motion can be derived from the kinetic energy and the potential energy of the associated links in the manipulator. The Lagrangian, L is given by (3). Since the manipulator is a planar one, the potential energy of the links are either constant or zero based on the reference plane. Hence, PE = 0. Using the Lagrangian, the dynamics can be derived using (4).

$$L = KE - PE \tag{3}$$

$$\frac{d}{dt}\left(\frac{\partial L}{\partial \dot{q}_i}\right) - \frac{\partial L}{\partial q_i} = f_i \tag{4}$$

Here, $\dot{q}_i$ is the ith task-space velocity and q_i is the ith task-space value i.e., x, y or θ. Here, f_i is the force or moment at the end-effector associated with the coordinates in the task-space of the manipulator. In order to obtain the joint torques/forces (τ), we use the Jacobian matrix derived in the previous section and the joint torques/forces are related to the task-space forces on the end-effector as

$$\tau = J^T(r)f \tag{5}$$

where, f is the vector of task-space forces/moments. The kinetic energy of the manipulator consists of the individual components of the kinetic energies of the bodies in the manipulator. Figure 2 shows the positions of the center of masses of these bodies which are comprising of the active slider blocks representing the active prismatic joints, the passive slider blocks for the passive prismatic joints, and the end-effector platform.

The Kinetic energy of the platform is been given in (6). The Lagrangian obtained from these energy terms was used to derive the dynamic equations of motion given by (4).

$$\begin{aligned}
KE = &\frac{1}{2}m_1\dot{x}_1^2 + \frac{1}{2}m_2\dot{y}_2^2 + \frac{1}{2}m_3\dot{y}_3^2 + \frac{1}{2}m_{s1}\left(\dot{x}_1^2 + \dot{y}_1^2\right) \\
&+ \frac{1}{2}m_{s2}\left(\dot{x}_2^2 + \dot{y}_2^2\right) + \frac{1}{2}m_{s3}\left(\dot{x}_3^2 + \dot{y}_3^2\right) \\
&+ \frac{1}{2}m_p\dot{x}^2 + \frac{1}{2}m_p\dot{y}^2 + \frac{1}{2}I_{zz}\dot{\theta}_z^2
\end{aligned} \tag{6}$$

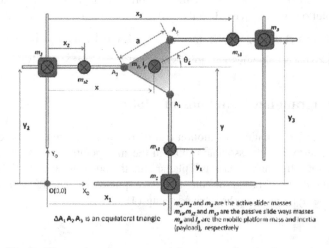

m_1, m_2 and m_3 are the active slider masses
m_{s1}, m_{s2} and m_{s3} are the passive slide ways masses
m_p and I_p are the mobile platform mass and inertia
(payload), respectively

$\Delta A_1 A_2 A_3$ is an equilateral triangle

Fig. 2. Kinematic parameters used for representing the Lagrangian

The expressions for the location of the center of mass of the bodies shown in Fig. 2 in terms of the task space coordinates are elucidated in (7). Here, the constant l_c is the offset distance of the center of mass of the passive slider blocks from the revolute joint locations on the end-effector.

$$
\begin{aligned}
x_1 &= x + \left(\frac{a}{\sqrt{3}}\right)\sin(\theta_z) \\
y_1 &= y - \left(\frac{a}{\sqrt{3}}\right)\cos(\theta_z) - l_c \\
x_2 &= x - \left(\frac{a}{2\sqrt{3}}\right)\sin(\theta_z) - \left(\frac{a}{2}\right)\cos(\theta_z) - l_c \\
y_2 &= y + \left(\frac{a}{2\sqrt{3}}\right)\cos(\theta_z) - \left(\frac{a}{2}\right)\sin(\theta_z) \\
x_3 &= x - \left(\frac{a}{2\sqrt{3}}\right)\sin(\theta_z) + \left(\frac{a}{2}\right)\cos(\theta_z) + l_c \\
y_3 &= y + \left(\frac{a}{2\sqrt{3}}\right)\cos(\theta_z) + \left(\frac{a}{2}\right)\sin(\theta_z)
\end{aligned}
\tag{7}
$$

4 The DeNOC Based Dynamic Formulation

The DeNOC - based dynamic formulation was done by first splitting the system into several open-loop subsystems as shown in Fig. 3. The constraints due to this cutting at the joints were modelled as Lagrange multipliers. The dynamic model of each of the PP subsystem was solved using the DeNOC based formulation and the final system was solved by combining the dynamic models of the individual (PP) subsystems and the dynamics of the end-effector.

By solving the combined system of equations simultaneously, the Lagrange multipliers were eliminated to obtain the joint torques/forces. The end-effector has been modelled as a floating body in the plane of the manipulator and is being acted upon by the Lagrange multipliers (λ_1, λ_2 and λ_3) which act as substitutes to the constraint forces due to the revolute joints at the ends of the legs.

4.1 The DeNOC Based Kinematic Constraints

The velocity constraints between the links in the ith subsystem were derived in the form of the DeNOC (Decoupled Natural Orthogonal Complement) matrices. The twist vector, $t_k = [\omega_k \quad v_k]^T$ for the kth link in the ith subsystem was written in terms of the twist vector of the $(k-1)^{st}$ link as

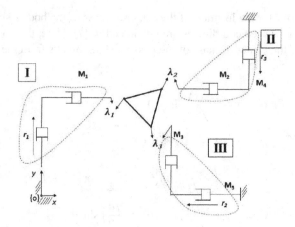

Fig. 3. The 3-PPR parallel manipulator with the kinematic parameters

$$t_k = A_{k,k-1}t_{k-1} + p_k\dot{\theta}_k \tag{8}$$

Where,

$$A_{k,k-1} = \begin{bmatrix} 1 & O \\ a_{k,k-1} \times 1 & 1 \end{bmatrix}_{6\times6}$$

$$p_k = \begin{bmatrix} \hat{p}_k \\ 0 \end{bmatrix}_{6\times1} \quad or \quad \begin{bmatrix} 0 \\ \hat{p}_k \end{bmatrix}_{6\times1} \tag{9}$$

$$a_{k,k-1} = [-a_k \quad b_k \backslash \sin(\alpha_k) \quad -b_k \cos(\alpha_k)]^T$$

Here, $A_{k,k-1}$ and p_k are the twist-propagation and joint motion propagation matrices, respectively. The term $\hat{p}_k$ is the unit vector along the direction of the joint axis and $a_{k,k-1}$ is the position vector of the $(k-1)^{st}$ link origin from the kth link origin written in terms of the DH parameters a_k, b_k and α_k[8]. It should be noted that the value of the joint-motion propagation matrix depends on whether the joint is a prismatic or revolute joint as expressed in (9). The complete twist vector t_i and the joint rate vector $\dot{r}$ for the ith subsystem are related in (10) using the DeNOC matrices. Here, $N_i = N_l N_{d,}$ and N_l, N_d are the DeNOC matrices shown in (11).

$$t_i = N_i\dot{r} \tag{10}$$

$$N_l = \begin{bmatrix} 1 & 0 \\ A_{2,1} & 0 \end{bmatrix}_{12\times12}, N_d = \begin{bmatrix} p_1 & 0 \\ 0 & p_2 \end{bmatrix}_{12\times2} \tag{11}$$

4.2   Dynamic Model of the Ith PP Subsystem

The equations of motion for each of the links in the subsystem can be written using the twist t_k, twist rate $\dot{t}_k$ and the wrench w_k as follows:

$$M_k \dot{t}_k + \Omega_k M_k E_k t_k = w_k \tag{12}$$

Here, $w_k = w_k^A + w_k^F + w_k^C$ is the total wrench vector comprising of the wrench due to the actuated torques/forces w_k^A, the wrench due to the external torques/forces w_k^F, and the wrench due to the constraint forces/torques w_k^C. The entire wrench vector is of the form $w_k = [n_k \ \ f_k]^T$, where n_k and f_k are the three dimensional vectors of moments and forces, respectively. The expression for the mass matrix M_k, the angular velocity matrix Ω_k, and the coupling matrix E_k are given in (13).

$$M_k = \begin{bmatrix} I_k & m_k d_k \times 1 \\ -m_k d_k \times 1 & m_k 1 \end{bmatrix}_{6\times6}$$

$$\Omega_k = \begin{bmatrix} \omega_k \times 1 & O \\ O & \omega_k \times 1 \end{bmatrix}_{6\times6} \tag{13}$$

$$E_k = \begin{bmatrix} 1 & O \\ O & O \end{bmatrix}_{6\times6}$$

Here, d_k is the position vector of the center of mass of the link from the link origin. Now, the equations of motion of the complete j^{th} subsystem can be expressed in a similar fashion as

$$M_j \dot{t}_j + \Omega_j M_j E_j t_j = w_j \tag{14}$$

Where, $M_j = diag[M_1 \ \ M_2]$, $\Omega_j = diag[\Omega_1 \ \ \Omega_2]$ and $E_j = diag[E_1 \ \ E_2]$. Now, the equations of motion can be converted to a minimal order equations of motion by pre-multiplying (13) by $N_d^T N_l^T$ and using the result that the power due to the constraint wrenches is zero making $N_d^T N_l^T w_j^C = 0$. After pre-multiplying and substituting for the twist from (10) and the derivative of twist, the equations of motion are expressed in (15).

$$I_j \ddot{r}_j + C_j \dot{r}_j = \tau_j \tag{15}$$

where the inertial matrix and matrix of convective inertia terms are given by $I_j = N_j^T M_j N_j$ and $C_j = N_j^T (M_j N_j + \Omega_j M_j E_j N_j)$ respectively. This model does not include the effect of the Lagrange multipliers which can be included as an external wrench. The final equations of motion are expressed in (15) where J_j^T is the jacobian for the jth subsystem.

$$I_j \ddot{r}_j + C_j \dot{r}_j = \tau_j + J_j^T \lambda_j \tag{16}$$

4.3   Dynamics of the End-Effector

The end-effector can be modelled as a floating body under the influence of external forces/moments due to the Lagrange multipliers. The equations of motion can thus be written in the form of translational and rotational equations of motion as expressed in (17) and (18).

$$I_f \dot{\omega}_f + \omega_f \times I_f \omega_f = n_f^E - \sum_{i=1}^{3} b_i \times \lambda_i \tag{17}$$

$$m_f \dot{v}_f = f_f^E - \sum_{i=1}^{3} \lambda_i \tag{18}$$

where, where I_f is the inertia tensor of the end-effector about the base frame O, ω_f is the angular velocity of the floating platform, n_f^O is the vector of external moments applied on the end-effector, and b_i is the position vector of the ith vertex of the platform (triangular) from the origin of the end-effector frame E. The terms m_f, v_f, f_f^E in the translational equation of motion are the mass of the platform, translational velocity, and the vector of external forces, respectively.

4.4   Complete Dynamic Model of the System

The equations of motion of the individual open-loop PP subsystems and that of the end-effector can be combined as shown in (17). Here, the joint torques/forces can be obtained by solving the system of equations simultaneously.

$$\begin{bmatrix} I_1 \ddot{q}_1 + C_1 \dot{q}_1 \\ I_2 \ddot{q}_2 + C_2 \dot{q}_2 \\ I_3 \ddot{q}_3 + C_3 \dot{q}_3 \\ I_f \dot{\omega}_f + \omega_f \times I_f \omega_f \\ m_f \dot{v}_f \end{bmatrix} = \begin{bmatrix} J_{f1} J_1^T 0_{2\times4} \\ J_{f2} 0_{2\times2} J_2^T 0_{2\times2} \\ J_{f3} 0_{2\times4} J_3^T \\ 0_{2\times3} - R_e b_1 \times 1 - R_e b_1 \times 1 - R_e b_1 \times 1 \\ 0_{2\times3} - 1_{2\times2} - 1_{2\times2} - 1_{2\times2} \end{bmatrix} \begin{bmatrix} \tau_1 \\ \tau_2 \\ \tau_3 \\ \lambda_1 \\ \lambda_2 \\ \lambda_3 \end{bmatrix} \tag{19}$$

Here, J_{f1}, J_{f2} and J_{f3} are matrices made of 0's and 1's depending on the torques/forces that are actuating the corresponding subsystem and 1_{2X2} is the identity matrix.

5   Validation of the Dynamic Formulations

In order to validate and compare the dynamic formulations, the joint torques/forces were calculated for the same profile which is shown in Fig. 4. The mass and other geometric parameters that were used for the calculations are given in Table 1.

Table 1. Manipulator Properties

Property Description	Property Name	Value
Side length of end-effector	a	0.2 m
Mass of slider (active)	m_1	2 kg
Mass of slider (active)	m_2	2 kg
Mass of slider (active)	m_3	2 kg
Mass of slider (passive)	ms_1	1 kg
Mass of slider (passive)	ms_2	1 kg
Mass of slider (passive)	ms_3	1 kg
Z – Moment of inertia (end-effector)	I_{zz}	0.5 kgm^2

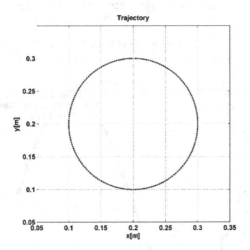

Fig. 4. Trajectory used for comparison

A circular profile was used for the validation. The joint/torque values that were obtained using the inverse dynamics formulations are shown in Figs. 5, 6 and 7. It can be seen that the values that were obtained using both the formulations exactly match. This was expected as the same platform parameters were used for both the algorithms.

While the Euler-Lagrangian formulation is energy-based, the DeNOC based formulation is vector – based but without the calculation of the constraint forces which are required in Newton-Euler formulation. Both the formulations provide same results as they should.

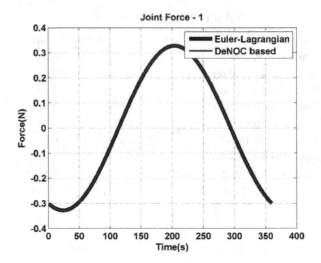

Fig. 5. Actuated joint force for 1ˢᵗ joint

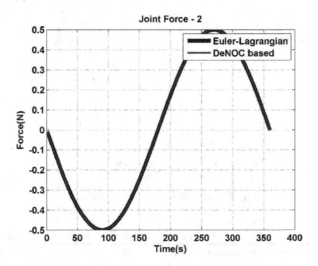

Fig. 6. Actuated joint force for 2ⁿᵈ joint

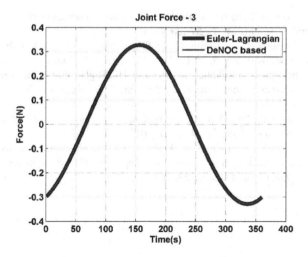

Fig. 7. Actuated joint force for 3rd joint

6   Conclusions

A planar parallel manipulator with 3-PPR configuration was analyzed and its' dynamics was studied by deriving the equations of motion using two different approaches. Both the formulations were validated using a simple circular profile and they provided the same expressions and values for the joint torque/forces throughout the trajectory. However, the usage of the DeNOC matrices for deriving the equation of motion eliminates the need for partial derivatives which are used in the energy based Euler-Lagrange formulation. Moreover, the pre-multiplying procedure followed in the DeNOC formulation removes the calculation of constraint forces required in the Newton-Euler formulation. Hence the DeNOC-based formulation is advantageous over two classical approaches namely, Euler-Lagrange and Newton-Euler.

References

1. Bonev, I.A., Zlatanov, D., Gosselin, C.M.: Singularity analysis of 3-DOF planar parallel mechanisms via screw theory. J. Mech. Des. **125**, 573–581 (2003)
2. Zhang, Z., Mills, J.K., Cleghorn, W.L.: Multi-mode vibration control and position error analysis of parallel manipulator with multiple flexible links. Trans. Can. Soc. Mech. Eng. **34**, 197–213 (2010)
3. Merlet, J.P.: Direct kinematics of planar parallel manipulators. In: Proceedings of the IEEE International Conference on Robotics & Automation, Minnesota, pp. 3744–3749 (1996)
4. Williams, R.L., Reinholtz, C.F.: Closed-form workspace determination and optimization for parallel mechanisms. In: The 20th Biennal ASME Mechanisms Conference, Kissimmee, Florida, DE, vol. 5, pp. 341–351 (1998)
5. Briot, S., Bonev, I.A.: Are parallel robots are more accurate than serial robots. Trans. Can. Soc. Mech. Eng. **31**, 445–455 (2007)

6. Hesselbach, J., Wrege, J., Raatz, A., Becker, O.: Aspects on design of high precision parallel robots. Assembly Autom. **24**, 49–57 (2004)
7. Bonev, I.A., Zlatanov, D., Gosselin, C.M.: Singularity analysis of 3-DOF planar parallel mechanisms via screw theory. J. Mech. Des. **125**, 573–581 (2003)
8. Saha, S.K.: Introduction to Robotics, 2e. McGraw-Hill Higher Education, New Delhi (2014)
9. Saha, S.K.: A decomposition of the manipulator inertia matrix. IEEE Trans. Robot. Autom. **13**(2), 301–304 (1997)
10. Saha, S.K., Shah, S.V., Nandihal, P.V.: Evolution of the DeNOC-based dynamic modelling for multibody systems. Mech. Sci. **4**, 1–20 (2013)
11. Yogesh, S., Vinoth, V., Ravi Kiran, Y., Mohanta, J.K., Santhakumar, M.: Inverse dynamics and control of a 3DOF planar parallel (U-shaped 3-PPR) manipulator. Robotics and Computer Integrated Manufacturing **34**, 164–179 (2015)

A 4PRP Redundant Parallel Planar Manipulator for the Purpose of Lower Limb Rehabilitation

Jayant Kumar Mohanta and M. Santhakumar[✉]

Center for Robotics and Control, Discipline of Mechanical Engineering,
IIT Indore, Indore, India
{phd1401103005, santhakumar}@iiti.ac.in

Abstract. This paper proposes a kinematically redundant planar manipulator for lower limb rehabilitation application, having configuration 4PRP. The challenges in the existing mechanisms has been analyzed and a new configuration is proposed. This configuration helps to improve the effective workspace of the lower limb rehabilitation robot. The lower limb rehabilitation systems are used to treat the post stroke patients and limb injured patients by providing rigorous exercises through the motor nerves recovery. This paper shows the advantages of the proposed 4-PRP kinematically redundant planar manipulator over existing 2PRP-2PPR in providing higher effective workspace with same capability in performing lower limb rehabilitation tasks.

Keywords: Parallel planar manipulator · 4PRP · 2PRP-2PPR · Lower limb rehabilitation · Redundant manipulator

1 Introduction

The parallel manipulators are better than their serial counterpart in terms of less error accumulation [1] but in reality, the parallel manipulator can be made stiffer without being bulkier. So, in this paper a kinematically redundant planar parallel manipulator for the lower limb rehabilitation applications is proposed. The lower limb rehabilitation systems are used to treat the post-stroke patients and limb injured patients by providing rigorous exercises through the motor nerves recovery. The proposed mechanism is a sitting/lying type rehabilitation system. This type has an added advantage over a body weight support (BWS) system in term of applications. Since in BWS requires the patient's body need to hang with supports. The patient who needs to be treated should be partially fit in order to undergo treatment using BWS system. However, the sitting/lying type (proposed system) can be used at any stage, even at the early stage (during the bedridden time).

The Motion Maker [2] is one of the commercially available sitting/lying type systems. It consists of two serial manipulators with three active joints in each manipulator (which are corresponding to hip, knee and ankle joints of the human lower limb). Another commercially available serial manipulator system is Physiotherabot [3], it has sensors to detect patients response. The above-mentioned systems are based on

© Springer Nature Singapore Pte Ltd. 2016
B. Vinod et al. (Eds.): ICAARS 2016, CCIS 627, pp. 53–62, 2016.
DOI: 10.1007/978-981-10-2845-8_5

the serial configuration which comes with error accumulation. In order to overcome this limitation few parallel mechanisms were proposed in the literature. Out of these, The Lambda [4] and the NEUROBike [5] (partially parallel configuration) are commercially available platforms. The commercially available The Lambda mechanism can be used as an exercising/fitness device and applicable for physically fit/normal humans due to the absence of orthosis and patient comfort systems. The improved Lambda like mechanism with orthosis and patients feedback is proposed [6], however, the system is bulky and the ankle joint requires a separate active motion arrangement. To overcome these limitations, a fully parallel planar manipulator namely 2PRP-1PPR [7] is proposed. However this mechanism had shorter ankle rotation range and the design modification has been done to increase the rotation range by using a gear train [8]. In this mechanism, the error accumulation is reduced, ankle rotation range is increased. However the workspace still got constraint, Therefore, to mitigate this limitation of workspace, this paper proposes a 4-PRP kinematically redundant planar manipulator.

2 Proposed Manipulator Design

2.1 Conceptual Design of the Proposed Manipulator

The proposed system comprises of a vertical planar parallel manipulator and leg orthosis. The conceptual diagram of the 4 PRP manipulator is shown in Fig. 1. The component arrangement of the orthosis and its conceptual diagram are shown in Figs. 2 and 3, respectively. The proposed parallel manipulator consists of four active prismatic joints as named in Fig. 1 as P1, P2, P3 and P4. The end effector is placed at intersection of linear guides connecting prismatic joint P1 with P3 and P2 with P4. Which rotates with the link connecting prismatic joint P1 with P3. The adjustable leg orthoses consist of three serial links in RRR configuration. In Fig. 3, the L_{thigh}, L_{crus} and L_{ankle} are shown as the links lengths of the orthosis, whose size can be adjusted to patient's limb size. While ϕ_1, ϕ_2 and ϕ_3 are showing the hip, knee and ankle joint rotations of the orthosis, respectively.

Here the knee angle is constrained to 0 deg to 90 deg, basically it is for patient's safety but at the same time it gives unique forward kinematics relation of the limb orthosis.

2.2 Design Modification

This manipulator has limited ankle rotation. To overcome this limitation a gear mechanism has been employed. This gear mechanism multiply the effect of rotation at the end effector. This leads to increase in effective workspace area. In this paper, the effective workspace is defined as the area in which the mechanism provide $-45°$ to $+45°$ at the end effector (which is also the ankle rotation for the leg orthosis). Mechanism with gear arrangement has been shown in Fig. 4. The proposed gear arrangement consists of four gears and formed an reverted gear train. The gears are mounted on the vertical linear slider. Due to this gear train the end effector experiences the rotation which is 1/G times the angle between the linear slider with horizontal. Here G

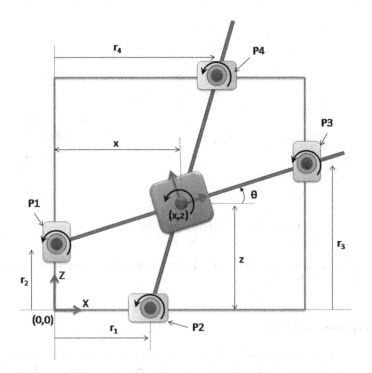

Fig. 1. Conceptual diagram 4PRP manipulator

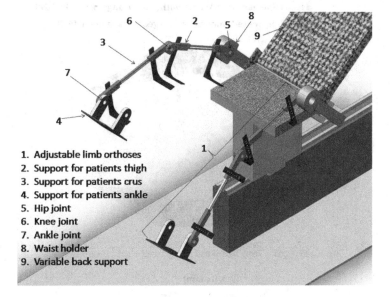

1. Adjustable limb orthoses
2. Support for patients thigh
3. Support for patients crus
4. Support for patients ankle
5. Hip joint
6. Knee joint
7. Ankle joint
8. Waist holder
9. Variable back support

Fig. 2. Leg orthosis with sitting arrangement

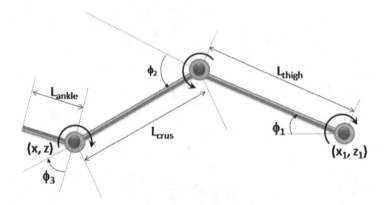

Fig. 3. Conceptual diagram of the leg orthosis

represents the gear train ratio. Since this is aiming to increase the source rotation the value should always be $G < 1$.

2.3   Workspace Analysis

To see the effect of implementation of gears, the workspace analysis has been done for the proposed manipulator. In this analysis, the effective workspace of end effector with

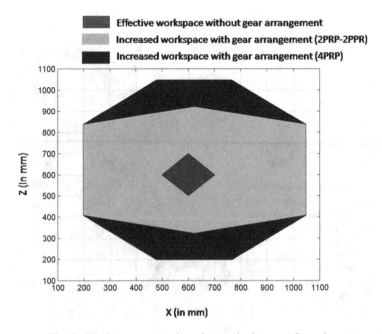

Fig. 4. Workspace comparison for manipulator configuration

and without gear arrangement are compared. For this analysis vertical and lateral distance between sliders of the manipulators are 1100 mm. Here G is taken as 0.25.

Workspace can be determined by using the forward kinematics of the manipulator. Forward kinematics for the 4PRP manipulator is given in Eq. (1) and forward kinematics of 2PRP-2PPR is given in Eq. (2)

$$
x = \frac{(r_2 s)(r_4 - r_1) + r_1 s^2}{(r_2 - r_3)(r_1 - r_4) - s^2}
$$

$$
z = \frac{(r_1 s)(r_2 - r_3) + r_2 s^2}{(r_2 - r_3)(r_1 - r_4) - s^2} \tag{1}
$$

$$
\theta = \left(1 - \frac{1}{G}\right) \tan^{-1}\left(\frac{r_1 - r_4}{s}\right) + \frac{1}{G} \tan^{-1}\left(\frac{r_3 - r_2}{s}\right)
$$

Comparison of results shown in Fig. 4, which clearly shows the significant increase in effective workspace.

$$
x = r_1
$$

$$
z = r_2 + r_1 \left(\frac{r_3 - r_2}{s}\right) \tag{2}
$$

$$
\theta = \frac{1}{G} \tan^{-1}\left(\frac{r_3 - r_2}{s}\right)
$$

This shows that in the presence of gear arrangement 4PRP redundant manipulator provide higher effective workspace than 2PRP-2PPR manipulator.

2.4   Kinematics of the Proposed 4PRP Manipulator with Orthosis

Generally the clinical gait pattern data is recorded in terms of the limb's hip, knee and ankle joint movements which are here represented by ϕ_1, ϕ_2 and ϕ_3, respectively. The forward kinematics of the leg orthosis is given as:

$$
x = x_1 - L_{thigh} \cos \phi_1 - L_{crus} \cos(\phi_1 + \phi_2)
$$

$$
z = z_1 + L_{thigh} \sin \phi_1 + L_{crus} \sin(\phi_1 + \phi_2) \tag{3}
$$

$$
\theta = \phi_1 + \phi_2 + \phi_3
$$

Where x and z are the positions of the ankle joint of the orthosis and q represents angle of the link L_{ankle} w.r.t. the horizontal in the x-z plane, whereas x_1 and z_1 are the coordinates of the hip joint. The Eq. 1 converts the gait pattern data to manipulator's end effector data.

Using inverse kinematics of the proposed 4PRP manipulator the actuators can be controlled to obtain the required trajectories. Inverse kinematics of the parallel manipulator is given:

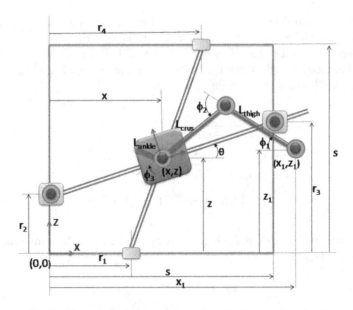

Fig. 5. Conceptual frame diagram of manipulator with orthosis

$$\dot{q} = J^+ \dot{y} \tag{4}$$

where,

$$\dot{q} = \begin{bmatrix} \dot{r}_1 \\ \dot{r}_2 \\ \dot{r}_3 \\ \dot{r}_4 \end{bmatrix}, \dot{y} = \begin{bmatrix} \dot{x} \\ \dot{z} \\ \dot{\theta} \end{bmatrix} \text{ and } J^+ = J^T \left(J J^T \right)^{-1}$$

Where J is 3×4 Jacobian matrix. Which can be derived using forward kinematics in Eq. (1). Task space can be derived using the gait data using Eq. (3). Using task space velocities the joint space velocity can further be derived.

This method is known as pseudo-inverse method. Using Eqs. 3 and 4 all the physiotherapeutic motion can be obtained by actuating the proposed mechanism. To demonstrate the effectiveness of the proposed mechanism and validate the mechanism, numerical simulations are performed with standard recorded gait patterns and discussed in the successive sections.

3   Results and Discussions

The proposed manipulator need to meet the requirements of clinical therapeutic treatments. In these therapeutic treatments the basic requirement is to provide directed motions to patient's limbs. Which are provided on a predefined trajectory. So the design must be feasible for providing motions required during the therapeutic

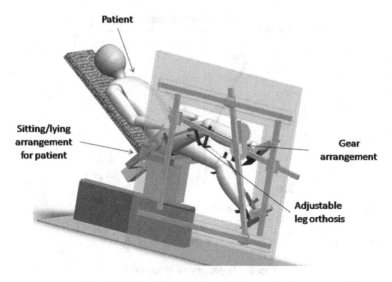

Fig. 6. 3D model of the complete mechanism

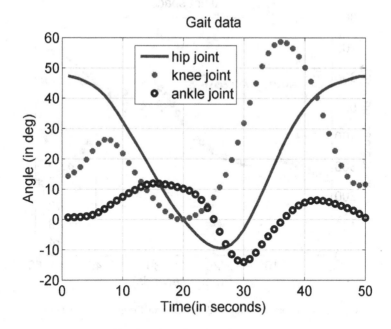

Fig. 7. Clinically obtained gait data

treatments. So, in this work the design validation motion capabilities are analyzed using simulations. Clinically obtained gait data is simulated using the proposed kinematic relations. This verifies that the proposed manipulator which can perform these motions within its workspace (Fig. 6).

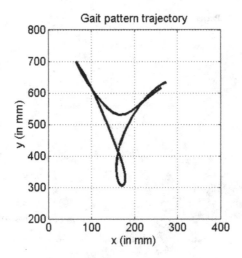

Fig. 8. Trajectory of ankle joint

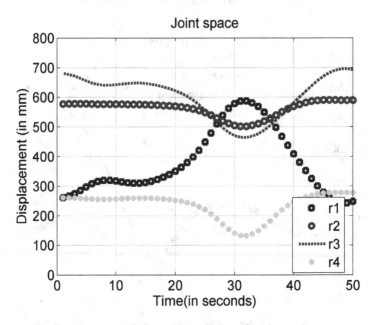

Fig. 9. Joint space of proposed manipulator for given gait pattern

The proposed mechanism contains four linear actuators. In Fig. 5 joint space variables are shown by the notation r_1, r_2, r_3 and r_4. In order to check real time implementation, feasibility and compatibility analysis, the clinically recorded gait pattern data have been considered for simulation analysis. This data in the form of joint angle rotations of hip, knee and ankle joints. Using this data actuator limits and workspace requirements are is verified. For the motion simulation three trajectories are taken. The simulation parameters are: L_{crus} = 400 mm, L_{thigh} = 410 mm, The distance between the actuators are same as in workspace analysis. Other than this the values of the constants are, x1 = 875 and y1 = 700.

Figure 6 shows the solid model of the proposed mechanism. Figure 7 shows the clinical gait data for the hip, knee and ankle joint rotations. Figure 8 represent the trajectory of the ankle joint and Fig. 9 represents the joint space required to perform these operations. The joint space displacement vector for these gait is obtained by using the Eqs. (3) and (4), the joint displacement profiles shows that r_1, r_2, r_3 and r_4 are well within 0 mm to 700 mm. These configuration is capable of providing necessary motion to the patient's lower limb to perform rehabilitation tasks.

4 Conclusion

In this paper the proposed manipulator, which is a combination of two mechanism one the RRR lower limb orthosis and 4PRP parallel manipulator has been validated for the execution of lower limb rehabilitation tasks. This architecture is completely parallel manipulator system while previous architecture were serial and partially parallel. Usage of this architecture is able to remove the actuators from the orthoses. The end effector rotation which was limiting the ankle joint rotation in the lower limb orthoses has been overcome by applying gear arrangement. This gear arrangement magnifies the ankle rotation which leads to the increase in the effective workspace of the manipulator, which is verified by the workspace analysis. This proposed configuration is giving higher effective workspace in comparison to the existing 2PRP-2PPR manipulator. The gait analysis shows that the proposed manipulator can very well execute the lower limb motions for rehabilitation purpose.

Acknowledgement. This research is funded by Council of Scientific & Industrial Research (CSIR), India.

References

1. Merlet, J.P.: Solid Mechanics and Its Applications. Springer, Heidelberg (2006)
2. Schmitt, C., Metrailler, P., Al-Khodary, A., Brodard, R., Fournier, M., Bouri, J., Clavel, R.: The "motion maker". A rehabilitation. System combining an orthosis with closed loop electrical muscle stimulation. In: 8th Vienna International Workshop on Functional Electrical Stimulation (2004)
3. Akdoğan, E., Adli, M.A.: The design and control of a therapeutic exercise robot for lower limb rehabilitation, Physiotherabot. Mechatronics **21**, 509–522 (2014)
4. Bouri, M., Gall, B.L., Clavel, R.: A new concept for parallel robot for rehabilitation and fitness: the lambda. In: IEEE International Conference on Robotics and Biomimetics, Guilin, China (2009)
5. Monaco, V., Galardi, J.H.B.S., Jung, G., Boccagni, C., Micera, S.: A new robotic platform for gait rehabilitation of bedridden stroke patients. In: IEEE 11th International Conference on Rehabilitation Robotics Kyoto International Conference (2009)

6. Mohanta, J.K., Saxena, C., Gupta, G., Santhakumar, M.: Kinematic analysis of passive sitting/lying type lower limb rehabilitation robot. In: 2nd International 17th National Conference on Machines and Mechanisms (iNaCoMM 2015) (2015)

7. Singh, Y., Santhakumar, M.: Inverse dynamics and robust sliding mode control of a planar parallel (2-prp and 1-ppr) robot augmented with a nonlinear disturbance observer. Mech. Mach. Theory **92**, 29–50 (2015)

8. Santhakumar, M., Mohanta, J.K.: A Rehabilitation Robot for Lower Limb Gait Therapy. Indian patent: 4757/MUM/2015 (Patent Pending)

Mobile Robotics

Development of a Mobile Robot for Remote Radiation Measurement

Ushnish Sarkar[✉], Surendra Singh Saini, Tumapala Teja Swaroop,
P. Sreejith, Ravinder Kumar, and Debashish Datta Ray

Division of Remote Handling and Robotics, Bhabha Atomic Research Centre,
Mumbai 400 085, India
{ushinish, sainiss, tejswrp, sreejithp,
ravinderk, dray}@barc.gov.in

Abstract. Remote measurement of radiation using mobile robots is recommended in nuclear installations. For this purpose various robots have been developed that carry a radiation sensor. However since the robot has to go very near to the source of radiation, the life of the robot's components is compromised due to high level of absorbed dose. We had earlier managed to increase the life expectancy of remote radiation measurement robots by allowing the sensor to be placed on an extendable telescopic assembly, analogous to a health physicist taking measurements using a Teletector. The first prototype developed had stair climbing capabilities but it was found to be over-dimensioned for various potential applications. A significant use of such robots is in taking measurements at nuclear reprocessing facilities having narrow cluttered pathways. This required development of a new version of the robot capable of negotiating the narrow pathways of such facilities. This paper describes the different aspects of the development of the mobile robot system with flexible radiation sensing capabilities.

Keywords: Radiation measurement · Mobile robot · Telescopic assembly

1 Introduction

Measurement of radiation is an essential task in order to record radioactivity in different facilities of nuclear industry. This task constitutes of continuous radiation profiling as in the nuclear reactor, and intermittent radiation measurement at different unplanned locations as and when required (usually when nuclear accidents and spillage occur). In the first case, Radiation Area Monitoring (RAM) instruments at previously planned locations are deployed. But in the latter case, usually health physicists and associated professionals travel to the area of interest and measure the radiation with the help of a Teletector. Although the Teletector can be extended, still the distance from the source has to be maintained in order to limit radiation exposure of accompanying personnel. However this results in poor localization of radiation source as well as errors in radiation measurement. In order to mitigate this problem, remotely operable robotic vehicle with onboard radiation sensor are required [1, 2]. The first prototype developed in Division of Remote Handling and Robotics, Bhabha Atomic Research Centre had

© Springer Nature Singapore Pte Ltd. 2016
B. Vinod et al. (Eds.): ICAARS 2016, CCIS 627, pp. 65–73, 2016.
DOI: 10.1007/978-981-10-2845-8_6

stair climbing capabilities[3, 4] but it came out to be over-dimensioned for most indoor applications. This required development of a compact version. The present version does have stair climbing capabilities. The subsequent sections of this paper describe the detailed development.

2 Principle of Design

The main driving force behind the development of the mobile robot with remote radiation measurement capabilities was to reduce man-rem consumption and facilitate increased access to hazardous location. But the environment that the robot may face, in most cases will be cluttered, and point of measurement will also not be planned. So, human in the loop control through tele-operation is deemed to be essential. Accordingly the robot has to be equipped with onboard cameras which will feed to a Human Computer Interface through which the operator runs the robot. So the following issues will be key considerations:

(a) Utilization of tele-operation technology
(b) On board radiation sensor for measurement of radiation levels
(c) On board cameras for feedback to the operator
(d) Wireless Communication link between the robot and Tele-operator station through which operator commands, camera image and, radiation sensor data and other system information is communicated between the robot and the Operator station.

In the subsequent section we describe the different aspects of system.

3 Robot Structure

A picture of the robot is shown in Fig. 1. The major structural components of the robot are described in this section.

3.1 The Wheeled Chassis

The robot consists of a wheeled chassis made of stainless steel. The chassis houses the battery, the electronics systems, the actuators and the drives. A rough survey of the potential places of application revealed that this system may be deployed for monitoring health of HEPA filter banks that form an essential facility in all radiological processing laboratories and plants. Accordingly, the dimensions of the robot were decided, considering the dimensions of standard HEPA filter rooms. However it should be noted that such considerations only made the design demands more stringent and in no way compromises the generality of the system.

Fig. 1. Mobile Robot with radiation sensor

3.2 The Radiation Sensor and the Telescopic Mechanism

Standard GM tube has been used as radiation sensor. The GM tube is mounted at the end of a telescopic assembly. A metallic tape driven mechanism has been designed to implement the extension and retraction of telescopic assembly. This entire mechanism (the GM tube and the telescopic assembly) can be rotated in Elevation and Azimuth. The motion in these 3 degrees of freedom – elevation, azimuth and extension-retraction effectively increase the reach of the radiation sensor.

It should be mentioned here that these 3 motions are tele-operable. The specifications of the mechanism are:

Extended length of Telescopic Assembly (max): 5 m

Collapsed Length of Telescopic Assembly (min): 1 m

Minimum Reachable distance from the ground (for the radiation sensor): 100 mm

Elevation movement range: −20° to +90°

Azimuth movement range: −90° to +90°

Figure 2 shows the different structural parts of the robot.

The different poses of the telescopic assembly are shown in Fig. 3. The robot vehicle also provides the mountings for the communication antenna and cameras for feedback to the remotely stationed operator.

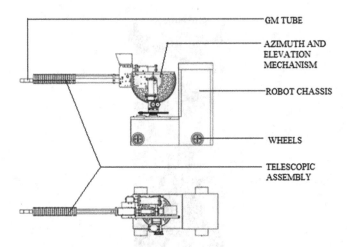

Fig. 2. Structural diagram of the robot with radiation sensor

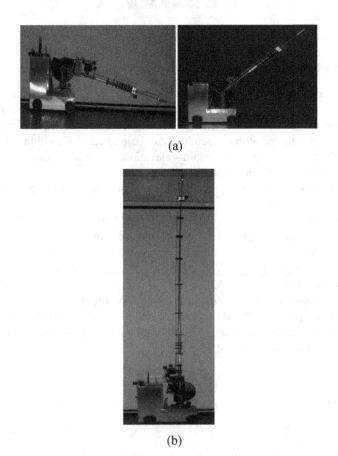

Fig. 3. (a) Different poses of the telescopic assembly (b) Extension of the telescopic assembly

4   Robot Control

The robot is controlled through tele-operation. A control station on four wheels houses all the RF equipment, a Desktop Computer with the robot control software, Control Joystick and buttons and also a UPS. Figure 4 shows the operator console. The remote terminal connects with the communication systems and receives data and images from robot and the radiation sensor. The movements of the robot and telescopic mechanism bearing the radiation sensor are controlled by the commands through the joystick or buttons.

4.1   Control System

The control system is distributed between the robot and the control station. Figure 5 shows the basic control system schema for the system. The arrows shown in the Fig. 5 do not necessarily denote direct plug-in and only represent the concept of interfacing. Different RF links are used for video and data communication between the robot and the control station. The following abbreviated symbols have been used in the control schema (Fig. 5):

T: Motor temperature sensor
B: Battery voltage monitor
RAD: Radiation Sensor
L: Left motor drive
R: Right motor drive
AZ: Telescopic assembly Azimuth motion drive
EL: Telescopic assembly Elevation motion drive
TA: Telescopic Assembly Extension-Retraction drive

In the system discussed here, the range of communication between the control station and the robot is 1 km Line of Sight.

Fig. 4. Operator console for controlling the robot and radiation sensor

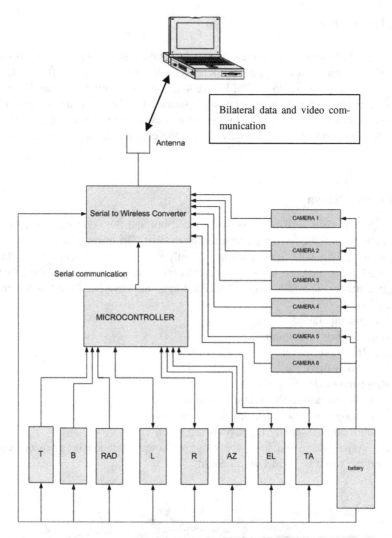

Fig. 5. Controller schema

4.2 Human Robot Interaction Design

Human robot interaction is one of the most important aspects for any tele-robotic system [5, 6]. Conceptually there are two broad pathways in this interaction—command - control pathway and feedback pathway. The commands issued by the operator are motion commands to the robot and the telescopic assembly. The command interface consists of joystick and buttons. The basic layout of the interface is shown in Fig. 6.

A set of 6 video images from onboard cameras are feedback to the operator from the remote robot environment to the operator thereby closing the tele-operation loops. 2 cameras are employed for watching left and right sides of the robot, 1 camera for watching the front of the robot, 1 camera for watching the back of the robot, 1 camera

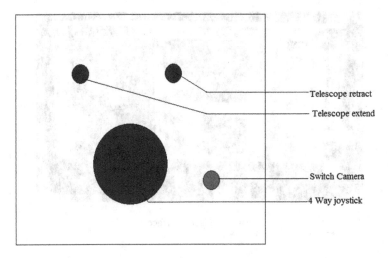

Fig. 6. Tele-operator command interface scheme

for watching the operation of the drive mechanism for the telescopic assembly, and 1 for watching the exact location of the radiation sensor.

1. User Interface

The user interface is shown in Fig. 7. The basic information facilities provided by the user interface are briefly described here.

- Camera view pane- The camera view pane at any point of time shows images coming from 3 cameras. The switch camera button can be used to serially roll through different camera views, as required by the operator.
- System Monitor- The user interface provides real time information about system related parameters like battery voltage percentage, motor temperature, left wheel speed, right wheel speed, telescopic arm azimuth and elevation, and length of the telescopic arm. Apart from these, the user interface also exhibits an application specific level exhibitor for standard HEPA filter banks representing the location of the radiation sensor in real time. The user can also set the different actuator speeds for robot wheels, telescopic assembly azimuth, elevation and extension through the UI.
- Radiation Measurement- Data from radiation measurement is available in real time to the operator through the UI. Both the sensor data and video feeds can be recorded on the remote terminal and facility to maintain Alarm set points are also provided. The UI also has the provision for report generation. The reports generated are detailed showing measured radiation data profiles along with date-time stamping and also link to the associated recorded session video file.

Fig. 7. User interface

5 Deployment

The system developed in DRHR, BARC is generic, but it has found its first potential usage in periodic health monitoring of the HEPA filters installed in the exhaust rooms of Waste Immobilization Plant, BARC. At present, trials are being carried out at the point of deployment.

6 Conclusion

The tele-operated mobile robot with radiation sensor provides a smart solution for ad hoc radiation measurement without risking unwanted radiation exposure of personnel. Presently such exercises are common not only among nuclear power and nuclear research practitioners but with growing threats of terrorism, security forces may also reap the benefits of such systems. At present, more agencies are being roped in for their valuable feedback post system-usage, which may lead to improved versions.

Acknowledgement. We acknowledge Zenn Systems for providing the industrial support necessary for the development of the robot's hardware and software.

References

1. Yin, Q., Gao, Q., Liao, H., et al.: Research on a kind of nuclear and chemical reconnaissance robot. Commun. Comput. Inf. Sci. **152**, 165–170 (2011)
2. Bogue, R.: Robots in the nuclear industry: a review of technologies and applications. Industrial Robot-AN International Journal **38**, 113–118 (2011)

3. Saini, S.S., Sarkar, U., Ray, D.D., Badodkar, D.N., Singh, M.: All terrain robot for remote radiation measurement. In: Proceeding of: 31st IARP National Conference on Advances in Radiation Measurement Systems and Techniques, At Bhabha Atomic Research Centre, Mumbai, vol. 1 (2014). INIS, IAEA, Issue 23, vol. 46
4. Saini, S.S., Sarkar, U., Teja Swaroop, T., Ray, D.D., Badodkar, D.N.: Development of technologies for remote surveillance and radiation measurement. BARC Newsletter Founder's Day Special Issue, paper 20, pp. 172–174 (2015)
5. Yagoda, R.E., Coovert, M.D.: How to work and play with robots: an approach to modeling human-robot interaction. Comput. Hum. Behav. **28**, 60–68 (2012)
6. Salvini, P., Nicolescu, M., Ishiguro, H.: Benefits of human-robot interaction. IEEE Robot. Autom. Mag. **18**, 98–99 (2011)

Development of an Amphibian Legged Robot Based on Jansen Mechanism for Exploration Tasks

Gopi Krishnan Regulan[1], Ganesan Kaliappan[1],
and M. Santhakumar[2(✉)]

[1] Department of Mechanical Engineering,
PSG College of Technology,
Coimbatore, Tamil Nadu, India
gopiregu@gmail.com,
ganesankalliappan@gmail.com
[2] Discipline of Mechanical Engineering,
Indian Institute of Technology Indore,
Indore, Madhya Pradesh, India
santhakumar@iiti.ac.in

Abstract. The paper discusses the development of a linkage based amphibian legged robot for exploration and surveillance tasks. The proposed system can walk on both ground and water surfaces. The proposed system has two major mechanisms for its motion namely a planar eight bar Jansen mechanism as a leg and an Ackermann steering mechanism as for turning. The performance of the proposed mechanisms is verified in terms of motion, force (motion/walking) and structural aspects. The effectiveness and performance of the system is demonstrated by using an in-house fabricated prototype for different working conditions. The Jansen legged mechanism is redesigned in order to improve the drag force during walking on the water surface.

Keywords: Amphibian robot · Jansen mechanism · Linkage kinematics · Parallel linkage · Structural stability · Exploration robot

1 Introduction

The ability of the robots which survives more than one environment is the popular topic among researchers. Living creatures which survives more than one condition of environment are called amphibians. Many bio inspired amphibian robots are developed in recent times. More number of research groups created platforms with the goal of inspiring operations of amphibious nature. For example, robot inspired from cheetah is developed in the laboratory of Carnegie Mellon University [1]. This robot has four legs and runs at 33 mph. There are robots developed which survive in rugged environments such as legged and crawling robots [2].

Sahai and Galloway [3] developed linkage structures for flying in the air using flapping mechanism inspired from the birds. The linkage structures are mainly used for the running on the rugged environment. Hexapods and RHex developed by

B. Vinod et al. (Eds.): ICAARS 2016, CCIS 627, pp. 74–91, 2016.
DOI: 10.1007/978-981-10-2845-8_7

Boxerbaum et al. [4] has flippers for surviving in the water and ground. Robots inspired from water striders are developed by using surface tension principle [5]. Basilisk lizards are developed for running on water using the drag force. These robots also can run on ground [6, 7].

In this paper, an amphibian robotic system is proposed which performs operations (survives) in two environments, viz. on surface of water and on surface of ground. The novelty of the system is a legged motion system for the amphibian robot. The proposed robot survives in rugged environment on ground and uses the buoyancy principle to walks on water surface. It is helpful in the exploration tasks in the forests with marshy or swampy areas (having water) and surveillance applications.

The remaining sections of the paper are organized as follows: In Sect. 2 – the proposed amphibian robot design is explained with its detailed specifications. In Sect. 3, the motion system design and analysis of the proposed amphibian robot are discussed. This section also describes the kinematic analysis, force model of the proposed system for walking on both ground surface and on water surface and structural stability of the proposed system. Section 4 describes the fabrication of prototype and control experiments of the proposed amphibian robotic system. Finally Sect. 5 presents the concluding remarks.

2 Design of Amphibian Robot

The proposed amphibian robot has six legs, inspired from the arachnid. Jansen mechanism is used to substitute the legs for running on water and on ground. The motion base (body) of the robot is inspired from the arachnid body in such a way that the middle legs do not collate with the front and rear legs. The middle and the rear legs are driven by single DC motor which has an encoder. This motor is fixed to the base with the special fixture, designed exclusively for this motor. The power from the motor is transmitted to the legs through the gears with the speed reduction ratio of 1:3.

The spherical Styrofoams are used as the feet for the legs to generate buoyancy when the robot runs on the water surface and it also helps in walking on the ground. The Ackermann steering mechanism is used for the heading (yaw motion). The front two legs are attached to the Ackermann steering mechanism and these legs are driven by two independent DC motors. The steering mechanism is operated by a servo motor which helps the robot to turn towards left or right.

The robot uses the tripod gait pattern to move in forward and backward directions. Therefore the legs connected to single driven shaft are 180° phase difference with each other to follow a tripod gait pattern. Due to this, the robot has more stability that the center of gravity can adjust within its triangular stability margin when it tries to roll or pitch. The conceptual design of the proposed system solid model is developed and presented in Fig. 1.

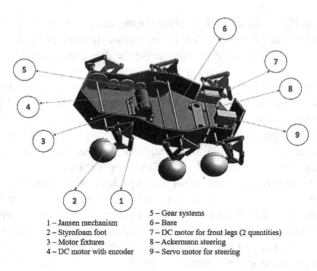

1 – Jansen mechanism
2 – Styrofoam foot
3 – Motor fixtures
4 – DC motor with encoder
5 – Gear systems
6 – Base
7 – DC motor for front legs (2 quantities)
8 – Ackermann steering
9 – Servo motor for steering

Fig. 1. The solid model of the proposed amphibian robot

2.1 Description of Proposed System

The specifications of every part of the proposed system are given in Table 1. Ackermann steering mechanism is used to turn the robot to the left or right direction. The steering is controlled by a servo motor. This steering is designed according to the base (body) dimensions of the robot system. The Ackermann steering mechanism dimensions are shown in Fig. 2.

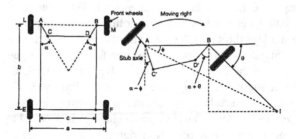

Fig. 2. Ackermann steering geometry and its specifications

According the labels given in the figure, the dimensions and the turning angle calculations are:

c = 215 mm, b = 325 mm, r = turning radius = 253.128 mm,

Table 1. Amphibian robot specifications

Configuration/component		Specifications
Length of the base		325 mm
Height of the base		65 mm
Width of the base		215 mm
Mass of the robot		1.24 kg
Shaft diameter		5 mm
DC Motor torque		1.36 N m
DC Motor torque (for front legs)		0.8 N m
Servo Motor torque		1 N m
Driving gear	No. of teeth	24
	Diameter	36 mm
Driven gear	No. of teeth	79
	Diameter	118 mm
Radius of feet		30 mm

$$\phi = \arctan\left(\frac{b}{\frac{c}{2}+r}\right), \phi = 36°(\text{maximum})$$

$$\theta = \arctan\left(\frac{b}{\frac{c}{2}-r}\right), \theta = 49.312°(\text{maximum})$$

$$\alpha = 14°(\text{Standard range of } \alpha \text{ is } 11.3° \text{ to } 14.1°)$$

3 Motion System Design and Analysis

3.1 Kinematic Model of the Proposed Leg Mechanism

For the leg system, Jansen mechanism is used since the robot can able to walk over obstacles or move in rugged environment. The Jansen mechanism has 8 links, 10 revolute joints and has only one driving link which corresponds to one degree of freedom. Jansen mechanism has one fixed link with one end offset by 15 mm in direction perpendicular to its axis. The driving link is connected to the driven gears through the driven shaft. It has five binary links and two ternary links. The end effector is a ternary link and the other ternary link is attached to one side of the fixed link. When the mechanism is working, the end effector of Jansen mechanism generates the trajectory. For getting higher efficiency to run both on water and ground surfaces, the trajectory must be changed so that it could generate suitable drag force when walking on the water surface. This can be verified by performing position analysis of Jansen mechanism.

The kinematic equations of the Jansen mechanism are derived using forward kinematic relations. The whole mechanism is considered as three four-bar mechanisms and equations are derived. The kinematic equations are programmed in the MATLAB

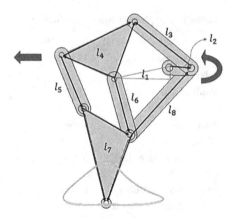

Fig. 3. Jansen mechanism with its default trajectory, (i) The straight arrow indicates the direction of motion, (ii) The curved arrow indicates the direction of rotation of driving link l_2, (iii) l_1 link is fixed.

software. Now the link lengths are changed to modify the trajectory path of end effector of the Jansen mechanism using trial and error method. The Jansen mechanism's vector diagram is shown in Fig. 3.

The Eq. (1) is derived by considering the triangle law of vectors and each four bar mechanisms is considered to have two triangle law of vectors.

$$l_{n1}e^{i\gamma_{n1}} + l_{n2}e^{i\gamma_{n2}} = l_{n3}e^{i\gamma_{n3}} + l_{n4}e^{i\gamma_{n4}} \tag{1}$$

where, $l_n e^{i\gamma_n}$ defines the position of the particular link end. 'γ' denotes the angle of links from the fixed position and 'n' denotes the link number. The end effector trajectory position is derived from the forward kinematic relations and it contains only links having numbers one, four, five and seven. 'w' defines the end effector position.

$$\begin{aligned} w =[&((l_1 \times \cos(\gamma_1) - (l_4 \times \sin(\gamma_4) - (l_{4,1} \times \sin(\gamma_{4,1}) \\ &+ (l_5 \times \cos(180° + \gamma_5) + (l_7 \times \cos(\gamma_7)), \\ &((l_1 \times \sin(\gamma_1) - (l_4 \times \cos(\gamma_4) - (l_{4,1} \times \cos(\gamma_{4,1}) \\ &+ (l_5 \times \sin(180° + \gamma_5) + (l_7 \times \sin(\gamma_7))] \end{aligned} \tag{2}$$

where, '$\gamma_{4,1}$' denotes first side of the ternary link 4 with respect to the fixed link 1. By plotting all the points for the full crank rotation, the paths of every link end is shown using MATLAB software in Fig. 4. The changed trajectory of end effector is also shown and the changed link lengths using trial and error method are shown in Table 2. The MATLAB code is given in appendix. The end effector trajectory shown in Fig. 4 is proposed to have higher efficiency when the robot runs on water surface as foot has more drag force to move forward.

Table 2. Link variables before and after changing its lengths

Link variables	Initial(mm)	Changed lengths(mm)
l_1(fixed)	38.792	38.792
l_2(driving link)	15	15
l_3	50	50
l_4	**41.5**	**40**
$l_{4,1}$	55.8	55.8
$l_{4,2}$	**40.1**	**42.5**
l_5	39.4	39.4
l_6	39.3	39.3
l_7	36.7	36.7
$l_{7,1}$	**49**	**45**
$l_{7,2}$	65.7	65.7
l_8	61.9	61.9

Note: The bold letter indicates that the link lengths are changed.

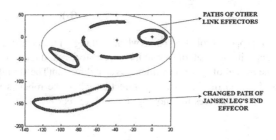

Fig. 4. Changed trajectory of Jansen leg by changing its link length

3.2   Force Model of the Proposed System

The force modelling of the robot is done separately for running on ground and running on water surface.

Force model of proposed system on water surface

The robot uses buoyancy force to run on water surface. The buoyancy will be generated if the robot walks on water surface due to the Styrofoam feet. Apart from buoyancy force, drag force will also be generated if it moves on water surface. When the feet move in same direction as the robot, the drag force will helpful for the movement of the robot. But if the feet move in opposite direction to that of the robot, the drag force will also act in opposite direction to that of the robot. Due to these two conditions, the submerged depth of the robot will be different for every second.

For finding the drag force (F_D), the coefficient of drag force is taken from the drag equation [6],

$$F_D = \frac{1}{2}(C_d \times \rho \times u \times A) \tag{3}$$

where 'C_d' is the coefficient of water drag (0.707), 'ρ' is the density of water (1000 kg/ m^3), 'u' is the velocity of foot and 'A' is the submerged area (Fig. 5).

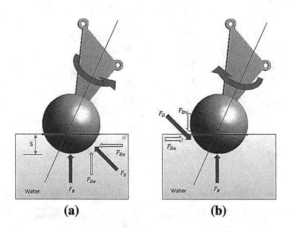

(a)   **(b)**

Fig. 5. Force model of proposed robotic system when walking on water surface, (a) The moving direction of leg is opposite to that of robot movement-forward direction, (b) The moving direction of leg is same as that of robot movement-reverse direction(The straight arrows indicate the buoyancy forces (F_B) and drag forces (F_D) direction when the robot is walking on water surface. The curved arrows indicates the moving direction of feet.)

The submerged depth (s) of the Styrofoam feet is not constant when walking on water surface. The submerged volume of the Styrofoam feet can be considered as spherical cup and volume of the spherical cup (V) is given as,

$$V = \left(\frac{\pi s^2}{3}\right)(3r - s) \tag{4}$$

where, 's' is the submerged depth, 'r' is the radius of the foot (25 mm), 'V' is the volume of the submerged volume of the Styrofoam foot. The buoyancy force can be calculated by multiplying the density of water with the volume of the submerged depth. The equation of the buoyancy force generated is,

$$F_B = \rho \int\limits_0^x \left(2\pi qr - q^2\right) dq$$

$$x = \begin{cases} s & 0 \le s \le 2r \\ 2r & s > 2r \\ 0 & s < 0 \end{cases} \tag{5}$$

where, 's' is considered as 'q' and integrated over 'q' with the limits '0' to 'x'.

The submerged depth has three variations. If the submerged depth is equal to diameter of the foot, buoyancy is the maximum. If the submerged depth is in between the diameter of the foot and zero, the submerged area is continuously changing and the buoyancy force generated will also be varying accordingly. If the submerged depth is equal to zero, no buoyancy force will be generated. Since, the drag force helps in generating additional buoyancy, the total weight of the robot will be equal to the addition of the generated buoyancy force and the generated drag force when walking on the surface of the water. 'W' denotes weight of the robot. Hence, the buoyancy force generated is given as,

$$F_B = W - F_D \tag{6}$$

The range of buoyancy force acts without the drag force can be calculated from the Eq. (5) and can be given in the range of '0' to '2.6712 N'. The range of drag force is from '0' to '0.7792 N'. Therefore the total maximum buoyancy force generated will be equal to '1.8920 N'.

Force model of the proposed system on ground surface (flat)

The robot uses the tripod gait for maintaining stability while walking. Hence, there is no chance of getting pitch motion and roll motion when walking on flat ground. But when it walks on slope both longitudinal and latitudinal, the center of gravity of robot is going to change its position. The stability margin is triangle for a tripod gait and center of gravity acts within the stability margin and there will be no instability. The stability margin for the proposed system is found out by intersecting the polygons generated when the robot moves with the tripod gait pattern and it is shown in Fig. 6.

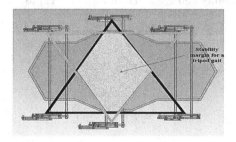

Fig. 6. Stability margin of the robot by intersecting polygon of the tripod gait pattern

The free body diagram for the robot when walking in longitudinal direction is shown in Fig. 7. The longitudinal stability reactions are derived by considering the standard acceleration of gravity, weight of the robot and the reaction forces and are given in Eqs. (7–9) as,

$$F = R_f + R_m + R_r \tag{7}$$

$$R_r = F\left(1 - \frac{L_r}{L}\right) - R_m\left(1 + \frac{L_r}{L}\right) \tag{8}$$

$$R_f = F\left(1 - \frac{L_f}{L}\right) - R_r\left(1 + \frac{L_f}{L}\right) \tag{9}$$

where 'F' is the weight of the robot acting in center of gravity of the robot, 'R_f', 'R_m', 'R_r' are reactions acting on front, middle and rear legs respectively. 'L_r' and 'L_f' are distance between the legs. 'L' is the total distance between the front and rear legs.

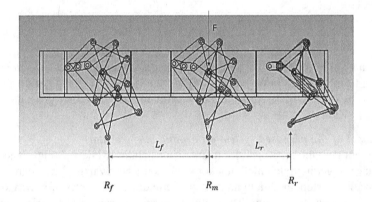

Fig. 7. Longitudinal stability reactions and forces when walking on flat ground

The free body diagram of the robot when walking in lateral direction is shown in Fig. 8 - front view and rear view. The lateral stability equations are derived as same as that of longitudinal stability and are given in Eqs. (10–12) as,

$$F = R_{fr} + R_{fl} \tag{10}$$

$$R_{fl} = F\left(1 - \frac{L_{fl}}{L_f}\right) \tag{11}$$

$$R_{rr} = F\left(1 - \frac{L_{rr}}{L_r}\right) \tag{12}$$

where in these reaction forces the first subscript represents which leg the reaction force is acting and the second subscript represents which side the reaction force is acting. 'l' is the left side and 'r' is the right side.

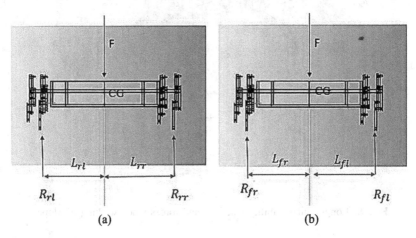

Fig. 8. Lateral stability reactions and forces when walking on flat ground, (a) front view of the robot, (b) rear view of the robot

Force model of proposed system walking on inclined ground surface

The free body diagram of a robot when walking on a ramp (inclined surface) is shown in Fig. 9. The stability reactions when walking on slope is derived as same as when the robot walking in longitudinal directions. The acceleration is need to be given for the robot when it is walking on slope. Therefore, the acceleration of the robot is considered as 'a_s'. The force 'F' acting on the robot can be resolved into two components 'F_h' and 'F_v' in the horizontal and vertical direction respectively. 'θ' is the slope of the ground, 'h_g' is the distance between the center of gravity and the ground surface, 'm' is the mass of the robot, 'g' is the acceleration due to gravity (9.8 m/ s^2). The reactions are given in Eqs. (13–16) as,

$$a_s = a_v + a_h \tag{13}$$

$$F = F_h + F_v \tag{14}$$

$$R_f = \frac{m}{L}\left(L_r(g \times \cos\theta + a_v) - L_f(g \times \sin\theta + a_h)\right) \tag{15}$$

$$R_r = \frac{m}{L}\left(L_f(g \times \cos\theta + a_v) - L_r(g \times \sin\theta + a_h)\right) \tag{16}$$

$$\tan\beta = \frac{L_r}{h_g} \tag{17}$$

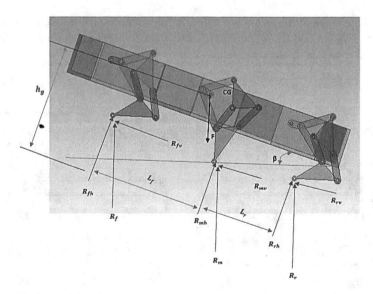

Fig. 9. Longitudinal stability reactions and forces when walking on slope

Equation (17) represents limiting angle for moving in the slope. From stability margin, 'h_g' limits are found as from 0° to 55°.

3.3 Structural Stability of the Proposed System

The structural analysis was done using ANSYS Workbench 14.5. For a tripod gait pattern, the robot will be standing on three legs when it is moving. The material of the leg is polylactic acid (PLA). Standard earth gravity is chosen. The entire weight of the robot is given for one leg and after the leg withstands the entire weight giving the von Misses stress value less than the yield stress. The structural analysis is shown in Fig. 10. The observed values of the maximum von Misses stress: 2.282 Mpa and yield stress for polylactic acid: 65 Mpa.

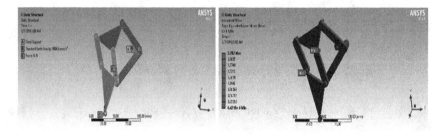

Fig. 10. Structural analysis of Jansen leg mechanism

4 Prototype of Proposed System

4.1 Fabrication of Mechanical Structure

The robot consists of base (body) which is fabricated using acrylic material since it is a light weight. The gears, motor fixtures, Ackermann steering linkage, Jansen leg linkages are printed in 3D printer using polylactic acid (PLA) material. The shaft and the revolute joints are made up of structural steel. The feet of the robot are Styrofoam material which helps to generate buoyancy. The motion system is carried out by the motors controlled by the motor drivers and Arduino with the help of sensor interfacing. The fabricated model is shown in Fig. 11.

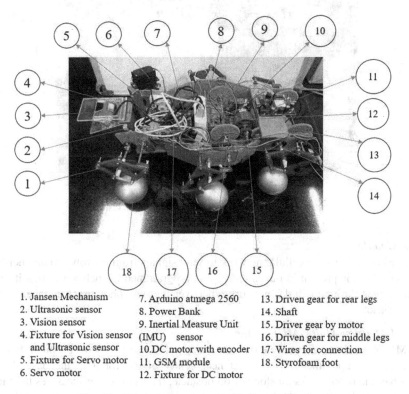

1. Jansen Mechanism
2. Ultrasonic sensor
3. Vision sensor
4. Fixture for Vision sensor and Ultrasonic sensor
5. Fixture for Servo motor
6. Servo motor
7. Arduino atmega 2560
8. Power Bank
9. Inertial Measure Unit (IMU) sensor
10. DC motor with encoder
11. GSM module
12. Fixture for DC motor
13. Driven gear for rear legs
14. Shaft
15. Driver gear by motor
16. Driven gear for middle legs
17. Wires for connection
18. Styrofoam foot

Fig. 11. Fabricated prototype with its specifications

4.2 Controller Details

The control of the robot is carried out by Arduino atmega 2560, GSM module, motor drivers and sensors such as vision sensor (high storage capacity camera), ultrasonic sensor and inertial measure unit (IMU) sensor. The robot is powered by a 12 V battery. The sensors setup connection is shown in Fig. 12.

Ultrasonic sensor

The ultrasonic sensor used will be helpful in finding the distances from the obstacles. The ultrasonic sensor has the capacity of detecting 2 cm to 4 meters and the angle detection of maximum of 13°. When any obstacle is detected with the range of one meter to 4 meters, it sends signals through Arduino control board to steer towards left or right. If the obstacle distance is within the range of half meter to one meter, then the sensor sends the signal to stop all the motors and the robot reverse the direction for half meters, then it turn towards left or right.

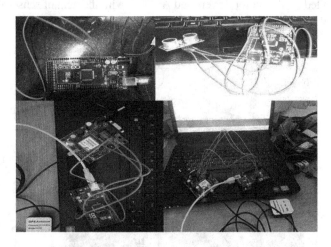

Fig. 12. Sensor setup and connection for testing

GSM Module

GSM module uses a cellular network to send signals from the robot to another SIM network which is present in our mobiles. It is programmed in such a way that it sends the messages through cellular network whenever the new photograph is taken by the vision sensor.

Inertial Measure Unit (IMU) sensor

IMU sensor has 3 axis accelerometer, 3 axis gyroscope (Y - yaw, P - pitch, R - roll) and 3 axis magnetometer. It is fixed near center of the robot to the base (body). Whenever the robot walks on slope or on obstacle, the gyro sensor measures the tilting of the robot in longitudinal or lateral direction and compare with the limiting angles and survive accordingly. If the limiting angle is about to exceed, the robot stops immediately. Then the robot reverses the direction and again it starts exploring.

4.3   Network of Sensor Setup and Controllers

The flow diagram of the sensor network and controllers is shown in Fig. 13. The logic used in sensor network is shown in Fig. 14. The main controller is Arduino which controls all other motor drivers and sensors.

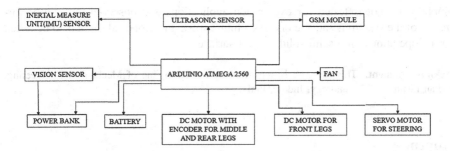

Fig. 13. Flow diagram of sensor network and controllers

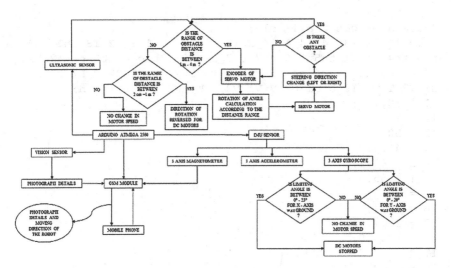

Fig. 14. Logic used in sensor network

5   Conclusion

The proposed linkage based amphibian robot is verified in terms of motion on both the surface of water and ground using buoyancy force and gravity force models, respectively. The structural stability aspects are investigated using a finite element method through ANSYS software. The kinematic analysis for the proposed Jansen mechanism was performed using the forward kinematic relations and the redesign of the Jansen mechanism has been performed by using numerical simulations of forward kinematics (simulations are performed in the MATLAB environment). The modified (improved) Jansen mechanism provided better performance in terms of improved motion trajectory and increased the overall efficiency of the proposed robot when it is running on the water surface. The in-house fabricated prototype of the proposed linkage based amphibian robot is tested for exploration applications and observed that the performance of the system is satisfactory. As a future work, the proposed robot is to be tested for its operations on a semi-solid ground surface.

Acknowledgment. This research is supported by the Discipline of Mechanical Engineering, Indian Institute of Technology, Indore, India.

Appendix

Kinematic Modeling of Jansen Mechanism simulation

```
close all; clear all; clc;
syms l1 l2 l3 l4 l4_1 l4_2 l5 l6 l7 l7_1 l7_2 l8 th1 th2
th3 th4 th4_1 th5 th6 th7 th7_1 th8 a b c a1 b1 c1 a2 b2
c2 a3 b3 c3 a4 b4 c4 a5 b5 c5 P P1 P2 Q Q1 Q2 R R1 R2 S
S1 S2 T T1 T2 U U1 U2 V V1 V2 W W1 W2 i j k l m n;
l1 = 38.792;
l2 = 15;
l3 = 50;
l4 = 41.5;
l4_2 = 40.1;
l4_1 = 55.8;
l5 = 39.4;
l6 = 39.3;
l7 = 36.7;
l7_1 = 49.0;
l7_2 = 65.7;
l8 = 61.9;
th1 = 105.135;
for th2 = 0:360;
b = (-(2*l1*l4*cos(th1))+(2*l2*l4*cos(th2)));
a = (-(2*l1*l4*sin(th1))+(2*l2*l4*sin(th2)));
c = (-l3^2 + (l4^2 + l1^2 + l2^2) -
(2*l1*l2*cos(th1)*cos(th2)) -
(2*l1*l2*sin(th1)*sin(th2)));
```

```
b1 = (-(2*11*13*cos(th1))+(2*13*12*cos(th2)));
a1 = (-(2*11*13*sin(th1))+(2*13*12*sin(th2)));
c1 = (-14^2 + (12^2 + 11^2 + 13^2) -
(2*11*12*cos(th1)*cos(th2)) -
(2*11*12*sin(th1)*sin(th2)));
i = (a.^2 + b.^2 - c.^2);
if i > 0;
th4 = ((atan2(a,b)))+(atan2((sqrt(a.^2 + b.^2 -
c.^2)),c)));
th4_1 = th4 + 90 + 45.817;
end
j = (a1.^2 + b1.^2 - c1.^2);
if j > 0;
th3 = (atan2(a1,b1)) + (atan2((sqrt(a1.^2 + b1.^2 -
c1.^2)),c1));
end
b2 = (-(2*11*16*cos(th1))+(2*12*16*cos(th2)));
a2 = (-(2*11*16*sin(th1))+(2*12*16*sin(th2)));
c2 = (-18^2 + (12^2 + 11^2 + 16^2) +
(2*11*12*cos(th1)*cos(th2)) +
(2*11*12*sin(th1)*sin(th2)));
b3 = (-(2*11*18*cos(th1))+(2*12*18*cos(th2)));
a3 = (-(2*11*18*sin(th1))+(2*12*18*sin(th2)));
c3 = (-16^2 + (12^2 + 11^2 + 18^2) -
(2*11*12*cos(th1)*cos(th2)) -
(2*11*12*sin(th1)*sin(th2)));
k = ((a2.^2 + b2.^2 - c2.^2));
if k > 0;
th6 = (atan2(a2,b2)) + (atan2((sqrt(a2.^2 + b2.^2 -
c2.^2)),c2));
end
l = ((a3.^2 + b3.^2 - c3.^2));
if l > 0;
th8 = (atan2(a3,b3)) + (atan2((sqrt(a3.^2 + b3.^2 -
c3.^2)),c3));
end
th4_1 = th4 + 90 + 45.817;
b4 = (-(2*14*15*cos(th4))-(2*15*16*cos(th6))-
(2*15*14_1*cos(th4_1)));
a4 = (-(2*14*15*sin(th4))-(2*15*16*sin(th6))-
(2*15*14_1*sin(th4_1)));
c4 = (-17^2 + (14^2 + 15^2 + 14_1^2 + 16^2) +
(2*14_1*16*cos(th4_1)*cos(th6)) +
(2*14_1*16*sin(th4_1)*sin(th6)) +
(2*14*14_1*cos(th4)*cos(th4_1)) +
```

```
(2*14*14_1*sin(th4)*sin(th4_1)) +
(2*14*16*cos(th4)*cos(th6)) +
(2*14*16*sin(th4)*sin(th6)));
m = (a4.^2 + b4.^2 - c4.^2);
if m > 0;
th5 = (atan2(a4,b4)) + (atan2((sqrt(a4.^2 + b4.^2 -
c4.^2)),c4));
end
n = (a5.^2 + b5.^2 - c5.^2);
if n > 0;
th7 = (atan2(a5,b5)) + (atan2((sqrt(a5.^2 + b5.^2 -
c5.^2)),c5));
th7_1 = th7 - 65.7;
end
P = [0,0];
P1 = 0;
P2 = 0;
Q = [(12*cos(th2)),(12*sin(th2))];
Q1 = (12*cosd(th2));
Q2 = (12*sind(th2));
R1 = -14*sin(th4) + 11*cos(191.6);
R2 = -14*cos(th4) + 11*sind(191.6);
S = [(12*cos(th2) + 13*cos(180+th3) + 14_2*cos(134.183 +
th4_1)),(12*sin(th2) + 13*sin(180+th3) + 14_2*sin(134.183
+ th4_1))];
S1 = 11*cos(191.6) - 14*sin(th4) - 14_1*sin(th4_1);
S2 = 11*sind(191.6) - 14*cos(th4) - 14_1*cos(th4_1);
T = [(11*cos(191.6)),(11*sin(191.6))];
T1 = 11*cos(191.6);
T2 = 11*sind(191.6);
U = [(12*cos(th2) + 18*cos(180+th8) +
16*cos(th6)),(12*sin(th2) + 18*sin(180+th8) +
16*sin(th6))];
U1 =  11*cos(191.6) + 16*sin(th6);
U2 =  11*sind(191.6) + (16*cos(th6));
V1 = 11*cos(191.6) - 14*sin(th4) - 14_1*sin(th4_1)+
15*cos(180+th5);
V2 = 11*sind(191.6) - 14*cos(th4) - 14_1*cos(th4_1) +
15*sin(180+th5);
W = [(11*cos(191.6) - 14*sin(th4) - 14_1*sin(th4_1)+
15*cos(180+th5) + 17*cos(th7)),(11*sind(191.6) -
14*cos(th4) - 14_1*cos(th4_1) + 15*sin(180+th5) +
17*sin(th7))];
W1 = (11*cos(191.6) - 14*cos(th4) - 14_1*cos(th4_1)+
15*cos(180+th5) - 17*cos(th7) + 17_2*cos(360+th7-90));
W2 = (11*sind(191.6) - 14*sin(th4) - 14_1*sin(th4_1) +
15*sin(180+th5) - 17*sin(th7) + 17_2*sin(360+th7-90));
end
```

References

1. Hyun, D.J., Seok, S., Lee, J., Kim, S.: High speed trot running: implementation of a hierarchical controller using proprioceptive impedance control on the MIT Cheetah. Int. J. Robot. Res. **33**(11), 1417–1445 (2014)
2. Prahacs, C., Saunders, A., Smith, M., McMordie, D., Buehler, M.: Towards legged amphibious mobile robotics. In: The Inaugural Canadian Design Engineering Network (CDEN) Design Conference, July 2004
3. Sahai, R., Galloway, K.C., Karpelson, M., Wood, R.J.: A flapping-wing micro air vehicle with interchangeable parts for system integration studies. In: IEEE/RSJ International Conference on Intelligent Robots and Systems, Algarve, Portugal, pp. 501–506 (2012)
4. Boxerbaum, A.S., Werk, P., Quinn, R.D., Vaidyanathan, R.: Design of an autonomous amphibious robot for surf zone operation: Part I - Mechanical design for multi-mode mobility. In: 2005 IEEE/ASME International Conference on Advanced Intelligent Mechatronics, pp. 1459–1464
5. Suhr, S.H., Song, Y.S., Lee, S.J., Sitti, M.: Biologically inspired miniature water strider robot. In: Proceedings of the Robotics: Science *and* Systems I, pp. 319–325 (2005)
6. Glasheen, J.W., McMahon, T.A.: Size-dependence of Water-running Ability in Basilisk Lizards. J. Exp. Biology **199**, 2611–2618 (1996)
7. Hsieh, S.T.: Three-dimensional hindlimb kinematics of water running in the plumed basilisk lizard. J. Exp. Biol. **206**, 4363–4377 (2003)

Adaptive Control

Investigation on Actuation and Thermo-Mechanical Behavior of Shape Memory Alloy Spring by Comparing On/Off and PID Controller for Precise Position Control

Tameshwer Nath[1(✉)], S. Karthick[1], Priya Chouhan[1,2], B.K. Lad[2], and I.A. Palani[1,3]

[1] Discipline of Mechanical Engineering, Indian Institute of Technology, Indore, Madhya Pradesh, India
tameshwer.nath@gmail.com
[2] Industrial Engineering Research Group, Indian Institute of Technology, Indore, Madhya Pradesh, India
[3] Centre for Material Science and Engineering, Indian Institute of Technology, Indore, Madhya Pradesh, India

Abstract. In this paper, PID controller is proposed to design in such a way that it can be able to control the input voltage as well as power to any load or electrical device not only manually i.e. through the computer but also automatically i.e. based on displacement. To evaluate the controller, an experimental set-up has been designed for investigating the thermo mechanical behavior of equiatomic Nitinol spring. Parameters such as load and position was varied and studied using a developed set up equipped with laser displacement sensor, programmable power supply and thermocouple connected to data logger. The control was superior while using PID controller for loads of 2.5 N and 3.5 N. Position control of 15 mm and optimum voltage of 3 V (4.073 A) was best suited with designed controller for more displacement PID controller is best.

Keywords: Smart material · Non linear actuator · Thermo-mechanical cycle set up · PID controller

1 Introduction

Shape memory alloys (SMAs) i.e. intermetallic compound are a type of smart materials that can be deformed at low temperature (Martensite phase) and regains to its original undeformed configuration when heated to a higher temperature phase (Austenite phase). Nitinol possess interesting properties in terms of high power-to-weight ratio, very large recoverable motion, great ductility, excellent corrosion resistance, stable transformation temperatures, high biocompatibility and the ability to be electrically heated for shape recovery [1–4]. These alloys have found its use in many applications such as actuators [5], micro-grippers [6], micro-pumps [7], instruments for minimally invasive therapy [8] artificial muscle, robotics and active control of space structures [9].

© Springer Nature Singapore Pte Ltd. 2016
B. Vinod et al. (Eds.): ICAARS 2016, CCIS 627, pp. 95–105, 2016.
DOI: 10.1007/978-981-10-2845-8_8

Utilizing SMA actuators in real applications will lead nonlinear behavior which requires complex control strategies [10].

The displacement control has been examined where accurate position control was an objective using various thermo mechanical cycle test bench (studies the properties of materials as they change with temperature) as displacement control is the primary objective, where as secondary objective such as failure due to overloading or over-heating [11] and the actuator's reliability can be of significant interest. The theme of the present study is to investigate the influencing parameters in controlling a Ni-Ti SMA spring. PID controller was used for the experiment and the influencing parameters such as load, actuation voltage, and control position has been varied and studied.

2   Experimental Set up

Experimental apparatus was established to model the behavior of shape memory alloy (SMA) actuator also to test the controller online. As Ni content increases, temperature decreases drastically so equiatomic (50 %Ni–50 %Ti) Nitinol spring (Dynalloy®) (Fig. 1)

- Coil Diameter = 5.86 mm
- Wire diameter = 770 μm
- Length = 13.86 mm (compressed)
- Activation Temperature = 90° C
- Max operating current = 400 mA
- Number of Turns = 18

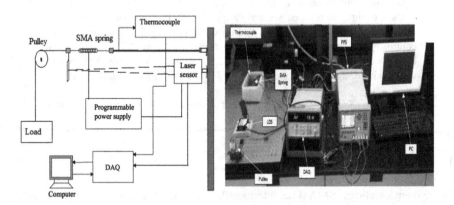

Fig. 1. Experimental set up (a) Schematic diagram (b) Actuator/Sensor location

The laser displacement sensor was connected to a 20 channel data acquisition system (DAQ Model: 34970 A, Agilent) and the scan step used for displacement measurement was 200 ms. A K-type thermocouple (200°C to 1350°C) was attached to the spring and the temperature measurements were recorded using DAQ. The actuation was carried out with DC Programmable power supply (Model: DP 1308 A, 80 W triple output, RIGOL) with a resolution of 0.5 mV/0.5 mA.

3   Control Parameters

3.1   ON-OFF Controller

The difference between desired output and current output is actuating error signal (*e*) that depends on the sign of *e* for control signal i.e.

$$\text{Input } U(t) = U_1 e(t) < 0 \text{ at on condition}$$
$$= U_2 e(t) > 0 \text{ at off condition}$$

In the current scenario, to control the position of SMA spring U_1 was set to 0 V and U_2 was varied as 2 V, 2.5 V, and 3 V.

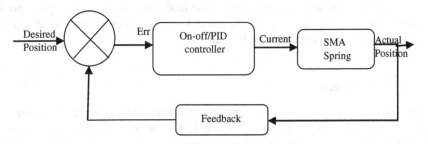

Fig. 2. Control architecture

Figure 2 shows the implementation technique of on/off controller which is used to control the displacement at required point.

3.2   PID Controller

The equation used for control using PID controller is –

$$U(t) = Kp.e(t) + Ki \int_0^t e(t) + Kd.de(t)/dt$$

In these equations, K_p is the proportional tuning constant, K_i is the integral tuning constant, K_d is the derivative tuning constant, T_i is the integral time, T_d is the derivative time, and error e(t) is the difference between the set point r(t) and the process variable c(t) at time t. The process of determining the parameters for PID controller K_p, T_i, and T_d to achieve high and consistent performance specifications is known as controller tuning. In the design of a PID controller, these controller parameters must be optimally selected in such a way that the closed loop system has to give desired response [11].

4   Result and Discussion

It should be noted that, even though the spring is compressing, the scales have to be multiplied with a common factor to have a zero reference and a positive scale for better understanding. It was observed that, while the spring was compressed during actuation, the values change from negative to zero. After changing the values to positive scale the reading indicates the control position at 10 mm, 15 mm and 20 mm which was observed as −10 mm, −5 mm and 0 mm.

To control the displacement during compression of the spring with respect to time and temperature, electrical heating of the SMA spring was carried out. Thermo mechanical cycles were performed by applying electric current at varying loads ranging from 2.5 N to 4.5 N and the return stroke was controlled at different lengths. Figure 3 emphasizes the SMA spring that is used as an actuator to lift the load for different loads [12]. For each positional control, the voltage and load is between text and figure should be about 8 mm, the distance between figure and caption about 6 mm. varied and the optimum parameters of control were investigated.

4.1   Without Controller

Heating and cooling for five cycles were recorded and analyzed for a maximum displacement attained without controller. Figure 4(a) shows the maximum displacement obtained and the control position selected according to the maximum displacement. Only two control positions for lower loads were selected as the spring returned to its

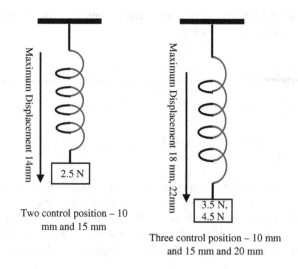

Fig. 3. Control positions and the maximum displacement obtained with different weights

initial compressed state. Three control positions were selected for 3.5 N and 4.5 N load. Figure 4(b) shows displacement versus time for the load of 2.5 N, 3.5 N and 4.5 N at 2.0 V. It can be observed from the Figs. 4(a–e) that the maximum displacement for 2.5 N were 14 mm, 18 mm for 3.5 N and 22 mm for 4.5 N respectively. Time taken to complete one cycle was 100 s (30 s for heating and 70 s for cooling) and the applied voltage was 2.0 V. Minimum voltage was taken to measure the maximum displacement and precise temperature preciously. The speed of actuation with different loads was not studied as it is beyond the scope of this paper. Figure 4(b) shows the time vs. temperature plot. The maximum temperature to actuate the spring was approximately 60°C, which was achieved for all the loads. There was a rather homogeneous temperature profile for all the loads and the loads did not have considerable influence. For one of the cycle, hysteresis (dynamic lag between heating and cooling cycle) graphs were plotted as depicted in Fig. 4(c), (d) and (e) at 2 V with 2.5 N load. During heating and cooling the displacement varies drastically approximate 40°C–50°C, which might be the temperature transformation. As a result, there is intersection as seen in Fig. 4(e), moreover there is a significant change is significant change which can be observed from Fig. 4(c) and (d) in the mentioned temperature region. Furthermore, once the spring compresses, the displacement clearly reduces more rapidly after 12.5 mm. However, the hysteresis loop was compact in all the three instances.

4.2   With ON-OFF Controller

Figure 5(a) and (c) shows controlled position of spring at 10 mm and 15 mm for 2.5 N and its corresponding time vs temperature graph is represented in Fig. 5(b) and (d). The experiments were conducted with three different voltages of 2.0 V, 2.5 V and 3.0 V. Only two control positions were selected as the spring returned to its original position. It can be observed from Fig. 5(a) that, at 2.0 V a maximum displacement of 12 mm within 9 s was detected, and the spring attained its controlled limit within 28 s. Further it returned to the control position in 44 s. The precise control was achieved at cycle time of 42 s. At 3.0 V, maximum displacement was 14 mm and it took approximately 67 s to reach the control position. In Fig. 5(c), spring is loaded with 2.5 N, and controlled at 15 mm, working under different voltages. All voltages are able to control the spring at 15 mm after 50 s from the beginning. The temperature profile for 10 mm control was varying from 45°C–60°C, and it increased drastically for 15 mm, where it reached 100°C but gradually reduced after the first cycle. It was evident that, at 2.5 N, 15 mm control was reliable with on/off controller.

At higher loads, one more control position was possible when the maximum elongation achieved. In Fig. 6(a) displacement versus time at 2.0 V is shown, where the displacement increased drastically. It reached 14 mm and then gradually reduced to 10 mm whereas at application of 2.5 V, displacement was 14.5 mm and it was not stabilized properly at 10 mm. There were fluctuations in displacement and temperature as the voltage was increased to 3 V. At 3.0 V, maximum displacement was 25 mm then it returned to 9.5 mm. The temperature profile is shown in Fig. 6(b). In Fig. 6(c), precise control at 15 mm is achieved at every voltages after 25 s, for that 60–70°C is required as depicted in Fig. 6(d). In Fig. 6(e) shows displacement versus time at

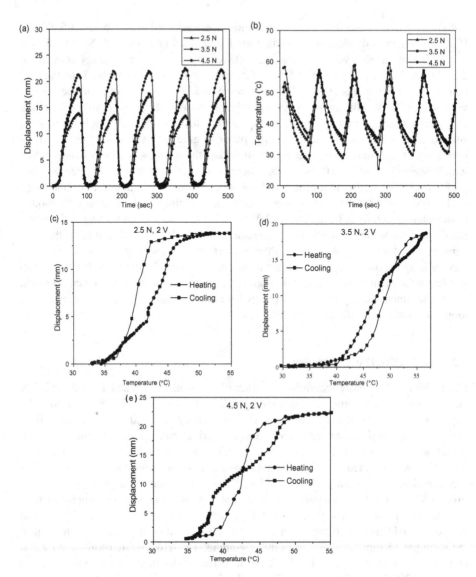

Fig. 4. (a) Displacement vs Time for different loads (b) Temperature vs time plot for different loads, (c) Response curve for 2.5 N, (d) Response curve for 3.5 N (e) Response curve for 4.5 N

voltage of 2.0 V, 2.5 V and 3.0 V. when spring is controlled at 20 mm with 3.5 N loads. It was observed that displacement is not precisely controlled as observed in previous study at 15 mm. Figure 6(f) shows that temperature is also fluctuating at that time. Therefore, 15 mm was precisely controlled for the 3.5 N loads with different voltages. Further increasing the load showed that the control was better as witnessed at 15 mm however, the temperature of the spring fluctuated.

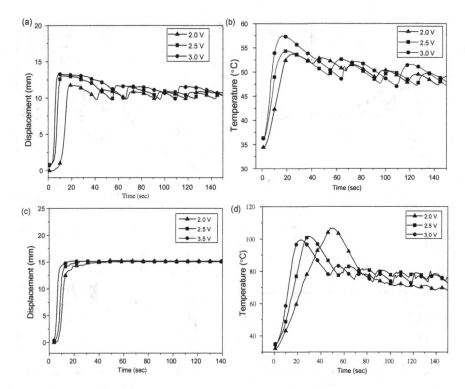

Fig. 5. Spring loaded with 2.5 N controlled at 10 mm, 15 mm (a) Displacement vs. time curve for 2.0 V, 2.5 V and 3.0 V when controlled at 10 mm, (b)Temperature vs. time curve for 2.0 V, 2.5 V and 3.0 V when controlled at 10 mm, (c) Displacement vs. time curve for 2.0 V, 2.5 V and 3.0 V when controlled at 15 mm, d)Temperature vs. time curve for 2.0 V, 2.5 V and 3.0 V when controlled at 15 mm

The load was increased from 3.5 N to 4.5 N, and three control positions were selected. The time vs. displacement graphs are shown in Fig. 7(a, c, e). Its corresponding temperature profile is plotted in Fig. 7(b, d, and f). Since displacement depends on increment or decrement of voltage fluctuation was observed as seen in Fig. 7(a), when the control position was 10 mm. The maximum displacement was 15 mm, 32 mm and 37 mm for 2.0 V, 2.5 V and 3.0 V respectively. In this figure it can been seen that at controlling time for 10 mm distance of all the voltages were increasing i.e. 20 s, 80 s and 100 s. However, control is not proper due to fluctuations. When controlling position was 15 mm and 20 mm, as shown in Fig. 7(c) and (e), controlling was not very precise, but it is time taken to gain the control position was very high. Temperature for all these cases was varying between 40–50°C due to difficulty in control.

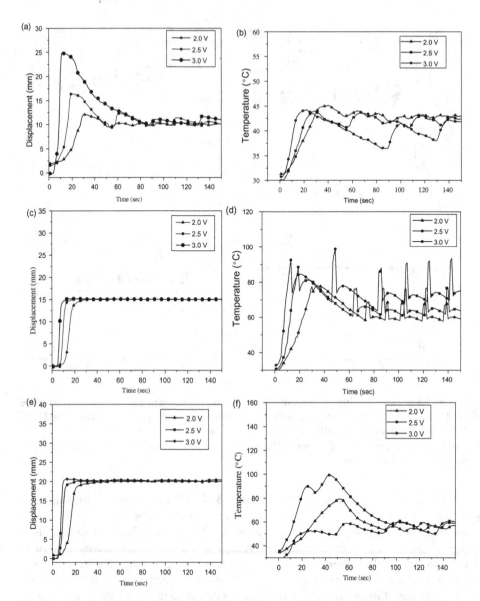

Fig. 6. spring loaded with 3.5 N controlled at 10 mm and 15 mm, and 20 mm for different voltages (a) Displacement vs Time curve for controlled position at 10 mm (b) Temperature vs Time curve for controlled position at 10 mm, (c) Displacement vs Time curve for controlled position at 15 mm, (d) Temperature vs Time curve for controlled position at 15 mm, (e) Displacement vs Time curve for controlled position at 20 mm, (f) Temperature vs Time curve for controlled position at 20 mm

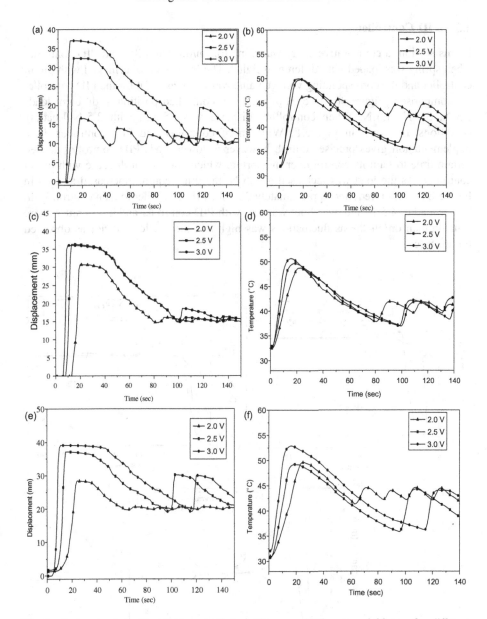

Fig. 7. Spring loaded with 4.5 N controlled at 10 mm and 15 mm, and 20 mm for different voltages (a) Displacement vs Time curve for controlled position at 10 mm (b) Temperature vs Time curve for controlled position at 10 mm, (c) Displacement vs Time curve for controlled position at 15 mm (d) Temperature vs Time curve for controlled position at 15 mm, (e) Displacement vs Time curve for controlled position at 20 mm, (f) Temperature vs Time curve for controlled position at 20 mm

4.3 PID Controller

In this section, a comparative study was done for on/off controller and PID controller when spring was loaded with different weights. The finest control achieved with on/off controller and the corresponding voltage value was taken as input for the PID controller for comparison. Figure 8(a, b, c) shows 15 mm controlled position at different loads 2.5 N, 3.5 N, 4.5 N. When controlling distance was 15 mm with 2.5 N Loading conditions as shown in Figure 8. With on/off controller and PID controller, both implementation gives precise control, however at lower loads PID controller needed certain time to gain its control over the spring, which was not in the case with on/off controller. As the load was increased to 3.5 N, the time required increased as seen in Figure 8 (b) and it required approximately 32 s for PID controller to gain control. With higher load of 4.5 N, the overshoot was less with PID controller and it was much more suitable than on/off the as fluctuations was high and the cyclic behavior as observed Figure 8 (c).

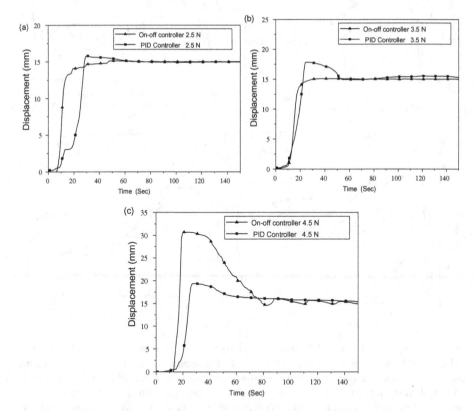

Fig. 8. Comparison of spring for on/off (3 V) and PID controller when (a) Displacement vs time curve when spring is loaded with 2.5 N (b) Displacement vs Time curve for loaded with 3.5 N (c) Displacement vs Time curve for loaded with 4.5 N

5 Conclusion

A comprehensive study has been done with varying parameters such as load (2.5 N, 3.5 N and 4.5 N), voltage (2.0 V, 2.5 V and 3.0 V) and positions (10 mm, 15 mm, 20 mm) to understand the thermo-mechanical behavior of Ni-Ti Shape memory alloy spring. The transformation temperature was found to be in the region of 40°C–50°C, as observed from the hysteresis plots. On/off controller was primarily employed for experiments. It was observed, the control was better at lower loads such as 2.5 N and 3.5 N with position control at 15 mm. Temperature of the spring was fluctuating during control because of release and absorption of latent heat. Other position control was not vastly precise with fluctuations at regular intervals. The results was compared with PID controller, where it was further demonstrated that on/off controller was advantageous than PID. Therefore a position control up to a maximum 5 mm can be realized with the help of on/off controller. However, with higher loads or larger elongation of the spring, requires PID controller to have a precise control.

References

1. Waram, T.C.: Actuator Design Using Shape Memory Alloys. Ontario Press, Canada (1993)
2. Degeratu, S., Bizdoaca, N.G.: Shape Memory Alloys. Design and Applications. Universitaria Press, Craiova, Fundamental Notions (2003)
3. Dolce, M., Cardone, D.: Mechanical behavior of shape memory alloys for seismic applications 2: austenitic Ni-Ti wires subjected to tension. Int. J. Mech. Sci. **43**(11), 2657–2677 (2001)
4. Nasser, S.N., Choi, J.Y., Guo, W., Issacs, J.B., Taya, M.: High strain-rate, small strain response of NiTi shape memory alloy. J. Eng. Mater. Technol. **127**(1), 83–89 (2005)
5. Ahn, K.K., Kha, N.B.: Modeling and control of shape memory alloy actuators using Preisach model, genetic algorithm and fuzzy logic. Mechatronics **18**, 141–152 (2008)
6. Lin, C.M., Fan, C.H., Lan, C.C.: A shape memory alloy actuated microgripper with wide handling ranges. In: IEEE/ASME International Conference on Advanced Intelligent Mechatronics, AIM, pp. 12–17 (2009)
7. Shahin, A.R., Meckl, P.H., Jones, J.D., Thrasher, M.A.: Enhanced cooling of shape memory alloy wires using semiconductor "heat pump" modules. J. Intell. Mater. Syst. Struct. **5**, 95–104 (1994)
8. Payandeh, S., Rothe, J., Parameswaran, A.: Design and development of actuating system for diagnostics application in minimally invasive surgery (MIS). Eng. Med. Biol. Soc. **4**, 2476–3473 (2001)
9. Barjibhe, R.B., Kumar, B.: Vibration control of cantilever beam using SMA springs in series. Int. Res. J. Eng. Technol. **2**(3), 1790–1793 (2015)
10. Sreekumar, M.L., Singaperumal, M.: Recent advances in nonlinear control technologies for shape memory alloy actuators. J. Zhejiang Univ. Sci. A **8**(5), 818–829 (2007)
11. Moallem, M., Tabrizi, V.A.: Tracking control of an antagonistic shape memory alloy actuator pair. IEEE Trans. Control Syst. Technol. **17**(1), 184–190 (2009)
12. Bhargaw, H.N., Ahmed, M., Sinha, P.: Thermo-electric behaviour of NiTi shape memory alloy. Trans. Nonferrous Met. Soc. China **23**(8), 2329–2335 (2013)

Vision System

Development of Automated Scanners for Underwater and Under-Sodium Ultrasonic Imaging

G.M.S.K. Chaitanya, Govind Kumar Sharma,
Anish Kumar[✉], and B. Purnachandra Rao

Non Destructive Evaluation Division,
Materials and Metallurgy Group Indira Gandhi Centre for Atomic Research,
Kalpakkam 603102, India
{chaitanyag,gks,anish,bpcrao}@igcar.gov.in

Abstract. This paper gives an overview of the development of automated scanners for underwater and under-sodium ultrasonic imaging of complex objects in two different scanning modes. The paper deals with the control instrumentation, mechanical movement, degrees of freedom and ultrasonic sensor deployed for the development of the automated scanner.

Keywords: Underwater scanner system · XY raster scan plan · θ-Z scan plan · Under-sodium scanner · Automated scanner

1 Introduction

Under-sodium viewing at high temperatures is an important requirement in sodium cooled fast reactors (SFR) for navigation during structural inspection. One of the major difficulties for in-service inspection and repair (ISI&R) deployment in SFR is the sodium environment [1]. As the sodium is opaque, ultrasonic inspection is the best suited method for carrying out ISI&R of the internal components of the reactor during shutdown period.

The recent advances in electronics and digital processing techniques have significantly improved conventional ultrasonic imaging systems and allowed new and sophisticated scanning methods [2]. Haviceslice et al. [2] describes how and why ultrasonic pulse-echo approaches are of substantial aid in medical field.

Voleisis et al. [3] focused on development of an ultrasonic imaging system for the Multi-purpose hybrid Research Reactor for High-tech Applications (MYRRHA). Focussed and unfocussed ultrasonic transducers of 5 MHz were used.

Sylvia et al. [4] described the application of Under-sodium Ultrasonic Scanner (USUSS) for Prototype Fast Breeder Reactor (PFBR) to detect any protruded part above the core plenum before starting the fuel handling operation. Images were obtained using under-sodium transducer of 1 MHz frequency mounted on a mechanical scanner.

Many demonstrated under-sodium viewing systems incorporate a single transducer with two scanning degrees of freedom (planar Cartesian coordinates in the XY plane) [5]. The XY raster scan plan provides constant angle perspective of the component. Imaging by XY scan plan requires complete coverage of the object. However, due to space constraints within a sodium cooled fast reactor (SFR), it may not always be

© Springer Nature Singapore Pte Ltd. 2016
B. Vinod et al. (Eds.): ICAARS 2016, CCIS 627, pp. 109–117, 2016.
DOI: 10.1007/978-981-10-2845-8_9

possible to deploy an XY scanner which may pose limitation for imaging large areas. This demands the development of a scan plan which can enhance the ultrasonic scanning span under space constraints.

Recently, Kumar et al. [6] have addressed the limitation posed by the conventional XY raster scan method due to the space constraints within the reactor and has shown the possibility of using θ-Z scan plan based approach for imaging of objects submerged in liquid medium. θ-Z scan plan is an alternative and this can easily be deployed even in constrained situations and still can cover large areas.

In addition to this many demonstrated under-sodium viewing systems incorporate a single transducer with two scanning degrees of freedom (planar Cartesian coordinates in the XY plane or cylindrical coordinates, θ-Z domain) [7].

To demonstrate XY raster scan plan and θ-Z scan plan, we have developed a 5-axes underwater scanner system. After successful implementation of this system, we have developed an under-sodium scanner for carrying out the θ-Z scan plan imaging in the sodium environment.

2   Automated Scanner Systems

2.1   Underwater Scanner System

This underwater scanner was developed for carrying out the XY raster scan plan and the θ-Z scan plan of imaging. The underwater scanner system comprises of an immersion tank and a 5-axes scanner (X, Y, Z, θ and Φ) controlled by LabVIEW based software. Figure 1 gives the photograph and different components of the underwater scanner system. The details of the immersion tank and the 5-axes scanner are given below:

- *Tank:* The size of the tank is 1100 mm × 1100 mm × 350 mm and it is made up of AISI type 304 austenitic stainless steel. The glass windows of 12 mm thick glass of size 900 mm × 250 mm are provided on the sides for clear view of the scanning process underway. The leveling screws and sprit level are provided to check the parallelism of the bottom level of the tank.
- All the five stages are stepper motor driven and are controlled by a PC. The X, Y and Z stage comprise of ball screw (C5 grade accuracy) and anticorrosive linear motion guides. The details of each axis are given below:
- *X-Axis:* This axis has a minimum translational movement of 0.1 mm with user selectable higher values in steps of 0.1 mm or more. The maximum scanning distance in this axis is 500 mm.
- *Y-Axis:* This axis has a minimum translational movement of 0.1 mm with user selectable higher values in steps of 0.1 mm or more. The maximum scanning distance in this axis is 500 mm.
- *Z-Axis:* This axis has a minimum translational movement of 0.1 mm with user selectable higher values in steps of 0.1 mm or more. The maximum scanning distance in this axis is 250 mm.
- *θ-Axis:* This axis has a minimum rotational movement of 0.1° with user selectable higher values in steps of 0.1° or more. The maximum rotation in this axis is ± 360°.

- *Φ-Axis:* This axis has a minimum gyration movement of 0.1° with user selectable higher values in steps of 0.1° or more. The maximum gyration in this axis is ±360°.

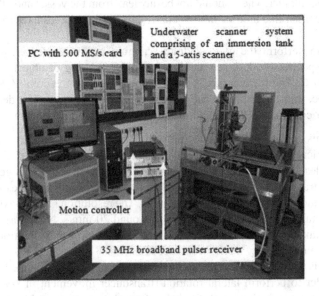

Fig. 1. Experimental setup for underwater ultrasonic imaging

For all the linear axes, scanning speed is in the range of 1 mm/s – 10 mm/s with user selectable speed range in steps of 1 mm/s. Repeatability of the scanner is very high with an error less than 0.02 mm for the linear axes and 0.01° for rotatory axes. Limit switches are provided for X, Y and Z axes to know the extreme positions of these axes. A feedback mechanism has been provided using rotary position encoder for rotary axis and linear scale for linear axis for accurate determination of the current position of all stages during scanning. Provision for display of position information is also provided.

A special holder is provided to firmly hold the cylindrical ultrasonic transducer during scanning. The maximum weight of the transducer that the holder can hold is ~150 gms. The holder is generic enough to accommodate different dimension sensors.

Suitable four axes motor driver and motion controller is provided. The motor driver make is NI MID 7604 and the motor controller make is NI PCI 7334. Good quality stepper motors are used for vibration free movement of the scanner.

Once the imaging was done in XY raster scan plan and the θ-Z scan plan using the underwater scanner, further imaging studies were carried out in the sodium environment. Since, this scanner is an underwater scanner for lab environment, an under-sodium scanner was developed to do experiments in sodium environment.

2.2 Under-Sodium Scanner

Sodium is significantly more reactive in air as a liquid than as a solid, and the liquid sodium can ignite at about 125°C. In a comparatively dry atmosphere, sodium burns quietly, giving off a dense white caustic smoke, which can cause choking and coughing. Hence, the under-sodium ultrasonic scanning of the objects has to be carried out in a closed vessel/container. There should not be any leak from the vessel and all the components of the scanner like motors, motion controllers, limit switches have to be on top of the vessel.

In order to perform the under-sodium scanning in θ-Z mode, an under-sodium scanner was specifically designed and fabricated for imaging of objects immersed in sodium at 180°C. The scanner has 3 independent degrees of freedom (Z, θ and Φ), an extension pipe, transducer holder and motion controlling devices. The details of each axis and other components of the under-sodium scanner are given below:

- *Z-Axis:* This enables the scanner to move the transducer mounted at the transducer holder vertically up and down. The traversing is done with the help of lead screw and linear guides. The axis is actuated by stepper motor with step down gear box. The maximum traversing distance in the sodium is 750 mm. Limit switches are provided to stop the motion beyond the specified limits. The resolution in the Z-axis is 0.1 mm. The maximum Z-axis movement speed is around 20 mm/s. Necessary precautions have been taken to make sure that the scanner is rigid, sturdy and vibration free during the Z-axis movement.

- *θ-Axis:* This axis enables the scanner to rotate the transducer mounted at the transducer holder to perform lateral rotation (transducer movement in x-y plane). The angular traversing is done with the help of revolute joint at multiple sections and supports at multiple points. The axis is actuated by stepper motor with step down gear box. The maximum angular traversing of ±90° is provided. The axis control for this traversing is done from outside the tank. The resolution of this axis is 0.1°. The maximum speed for this axis is 20 rpm.

- *Motion controller:* Suitable 3 axes motor driver and motor controller were used for scanning the objects. An in house, LabVIEW based programs were developed for controlling all the axis of the scanner.

The scanner was mounted on top of a sodium vessel and only the transducer, its allied holding structures and manipulative mechanisms were allowed inside the sodium tank through the spinner tube.

All components which go inside the tank were made of stainless steel (316 L/304 L) and same material was used for welding consumables. No parts in the scanner which were inside the tank and exposed to sodium were allowed to slide or rub against each other. The maximum weight that the scanner can handle is about 2 kg. To have hassle free operation stepper motors with appropriate torque were included. Weight of the scanner is less than 100 kg. Figure 2 gives the photo of the under-sodium scanner system developed.

Fig. 2. Under-sodium ultrasonic scanner

3   Underwater and Under-Sodium Scanning Mechanism

3.1   Underwater Scanning Mechanism

The specimen is kept in the immersion tank filled with water, and the probe is positioned and oriented properly using the transducer holder. Two scanning modes have been performed for imaging of the objects. The ultrasonic signals were acquired using a 5 MHz narrowband immersion transducer. A 35 MHz broadband pulser-receiver (M/s Panametrics, USA) was used for carrying out the ultrasonic measurements. The ultrasonic waveforms were digitized at 50 MS/s using a PCI based digitizer (M/s. Acquiris, 500 MHz) and were stored in ASCII format using a LabVIEW program. The details of the two modes of scan plans are given below:

1. XY Raster Scan plan. Ultrasonic imaging is commonly performed using raster scanning method with a single transducer having two degrees of freedom in the XY plane. It provides a constant angle perspective of the component. In this scan plan, ultrasonic beam is always perpendicular to the scan plane. Hence, a uniform time of flight based gate selection provides an ultrasonic image of any plane parallel to the scan plane. For example, for generating an image corresponding to the AB plane in Fig. 3a, time of flight of ultrasonic wave corresponding to PA (=P'B) should be selected in all the ultrasonic signals acquired. However, imaging by XY scan requires that the translation span should be equal to the extent of the object to be imaged, which is not possible always due to the space constraints. This constraint can be overcome by using the θ-Z scan plan.

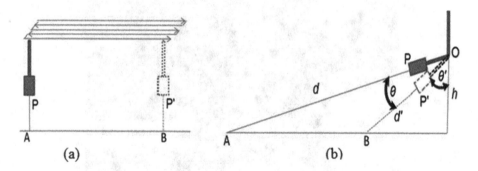

Fig. 3. Schematic of the (a) XY raster scan plan and (b) θ-Z scan plan

2. θ-Z Scan Plan. In this, scanning is done in the θ-Z domain. This provides a wide angle image and can cover large areas with much less physical movement of the probe. However, the distance of the probe from the object plane changes with the angle in the θ-Z scan plan. To scan the same plane AB using θ-Z based imaging (Fig. 3b), the probe pivoted at O, will be scanned from P' to P through an angle θ. Thus, the distance between the transducer P and the object plane varies from

$$d' = h * sec(\theta') - p \, at \, B \, to \qquad (1)$$

$$d = h * sec(\theta' + \theta) - p \, at \, A, \qquad (2)$$

$$where \, p = OP' = OP \qquad (3)$$

Accordingly, the correction in the time of flight selection has to be implemented in the software for θ-Z scan plan. Further, the distance along the AB plane also needs to be corrected as a function of the angle. Accordingly, the distance correction is also implemented in the software. The acquired signals were processed using the developed software for generating C-scan image slices corresponding to different planes oriented at different angles. The C-scan slices were then ensembled to generate the 3D images, after applying suitable corrections for the angle at different depths, for enhanced viewing of the objects.

Specific software was developed in LabVIEW for visualization of objects in the form of C-scan images and 3D images. In addition, the 3D isometric view images are also generated, using ImageJ© software by stacking various C-scan slice images generated by an in-house software developed in LabVIEW. The methodology and software developed for processing the data acquired by using the θ-Z scan plan is validated by quantitative measurement of various distances and depths.

3.2 Under-Sodium Scanning Mechanism

The scanning mode in this mechanism is θ-Z scan plan as explained in Sect. 3.A.(2). The under-sodium scanner was mounted on the top of a cylindrical vessel (sodium vessel) of 1.2 m diameter. A seamless pipe was used as spinner tube. The transducers were mounted at the bottom of the spinner tube with special arrangement. The movement of the spinner tube was controlled by stepper motors. The leak tightness of the scanner system was ensured by metallic O-rings. The entire scanner controlling motors were mounted at the top of the vessel and only seamless extension pipe and the transducers were exposed to sodium. The limit switches were used to restrict the maximum movement of transducers in vertical and angular directions. The scanner axes were calibrated with dial gauge before inserting into the sodium vessel. The software controlled motion controller was used for precise axes movements.

4 Underwater Ultrasonic Imaging

Figure 4 show the schematic representation of XY and θ-Z scan plan modes in the underwater experiment. For this experiment, a pliers was placed on the floor of the tank

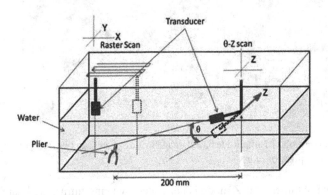

Fig. 4. Schematic representation of XY and θ-Z scan modes in the underwater scanner system.

and it was imaged in both the XY and θ-Z scan plans as mentioned in the Sects. 2.A.(1) & II.A.(2) respectively. The ultrasonic signals were acquired using a 5 MHz narrowband immersion transducer. A 35 MHz broadband pulser-receiver (M/s Panametrics, USA) was used for carrying out the ultrasonic measurements. The scenario corresponds to ultrasonic imaging of a tool fallen on the floor of a vessel.

Figure 5a shows the photograph of the pliers used for ultrasonic imaging. Figure 5b shows the ultrasonic amplitude based c-scan image of the pliers in XY raster scan plan. Figure 5c shows the ultrasonic amplitude based C-scan image of the same pliers, generated using the θ-Z mode after applying the above mentioned corrections.

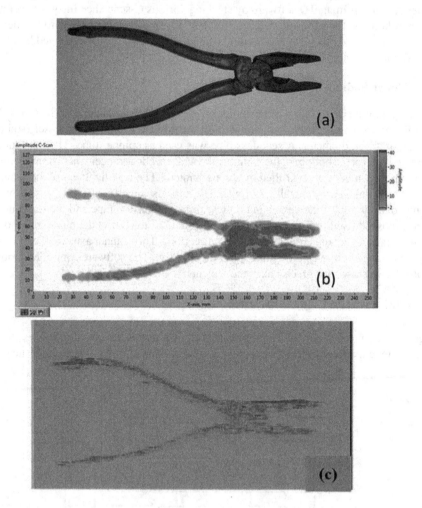

Fig. 5. (a) Photograph, (b) amplitude based image in XY raster scan plan and (c) amplitude based image in θ-Z scan plan, of pliers

The image obtained in θ-Z mode is generated by using ultrasonic beam at different angles of incidence and at a larger probe to object distance as compared to that in the raster scan mode. Still, various features of the plier could be deciphered. The amplitude distribution in each of the images reveals nearly flat regions facing the probe during scanning.

5 Conclusion

Underwater and under-sodium scanners have been developed and successfully demonstrated for imaging of various objects in the XY raster scan plan mode and the θ-Z scan plan mode. It is also demonstrated that the XY rater scan plan is more space constraint that the θ-Z scan plan. We successfully deployed the under-sodium scanner for imaging of objects in the sodium environment.

Acknowledgment. The authors are thankful to Mr. M.V. Vignesh of M/s Trotix, Chennai for the fabrication of 5-axes scanner and the under-sodium scanner. Thanks are also due to the colleagues of Fast Reactor Technology Group (FRTG), IGCAR for their support in carrying out the under-sodium experiments in their facilities. Authors thank Dr. C. Babu Rao, Raja Ramanna Fellow and Dr. T. Jayakumar former Director, Materials and Metallurgy Group, IGCAR for many useful discussions.

References

1. Sibilo, J., Breuil, E., Baqué, F., Augem, J.M.: Generation IV nuclear reactors: strategy and challenges of R&D program for improving inspection and repair of sodium cooled systems. In: Proceedings of the International Congress on Advances in Nuclear Power Plants (ICAPP 2010), San Diego, Calif, USA, Paper 8096, June 2010
2. Haviceslice, J.F., Taenzer, J.C.: Medical ultrasonic imaging: An over view of principles and instrumentation. In: Proceedings IEEE, April 1979
3. Kazys, R., Voleisis, A., Sliteris, R., Mazeika, L., Van Nieuwenhove, R., Kupschus, P., Hamid, A.A.: High temperature ultrasonic transducers for imaging and measurements in a Liquid Pb/Bi Eutectic Alloy. IEEE Trans. Ultrason. Ferroelectrics Freq. Contr. **52**(4), 525–537 (2005)
4. Sylvia, J.I., Jeyan, M.R., Anbucheliyan, M., Asokane, C., Rajan Babu, V., Babu, B., Rajan, K.K., Velusamy, K., Jayakumar, T.: Ultrasonic imaging of projected components of PFBR. Indira Gandhi Centre for Atomic Research, Kalpakkam 603 102, Tamil Nadu, India Nuclear Engineering and Design vol. 258, pp. 266–274 (2013)
5. Hans, R., Kranz, E., Weiss, H.: Under-sodium viewing – a method to identify objects in an opaque medium. In: Liquid Metal Engineering and Technology: vol. 1, Proceedings of the Third International Conference, pp. 419–421. April 9–13, 1984, London, England. British Nuclear Energy Society (1984)
6. Kumar, A., Sharma, G.K., Babu Rao, C., Purnachandra Rao, B., Jayakumar, T., Gobillot, G., Le Bourdais, F.: Undersodium imaging of SFR internals-simulation studies in water. In: Proceedings of ANIMMA 2013 Conference, Paper no. 1253 (2013)
7. Griffin, J.W., Bond, L.J., Peters, T.J., Denslow, K.M., Posakony, G.J., Sheen, S.H., Chien, H.T., Raptis, A.C.: Under-sodium viewing: a review of ultrasonic imaging technology for liquid metal fast reactors. PNNL-18292, March 2009, Pacific Northwest National Laboratory, USA (2009)

Smart Materials

Soft Robotic Skin from Intelligent Meta-Materials

Richard M. Voyles[1], Praveen Abbaraju[1], Daniel Leon-Salas[1],
Shree Sanjana[2], and Anush Lakshmanan[2(✉)]

[1] Purdue Polytechnic Institute, Purdue University, West Lafayette, IN, USA
{rvoyles,abbaraju}@purdue.edu
[2] Department of Robotics and Automation Engineering, PSG College of Technology,
Coimbatore, India
anushvv@gmail.com

Abstract. Smart product design has traditionally focused on design paradigms that facilitate the design of mechanisms with attached sensing, attached computation and attached actuation. The field of meta-materials, on the other hand, investigates imbuing materials with novel characteristics, such as sensing, intrinsically to the material. Structured Computational Polymers (SCP) are proposed intelligent meta-materials that combine sensing, cognition, and actuation into bulk materials, bridging the gap between novel material characteristics and integrated design paradigms. This paper describes the development of a flexible polymer meta-material that embeds a neuromorphic architecture for computation based on printable organic semiconductors with intrinsic pressure sensing co-designed with an algorithm to compute the centroid of pressure. Based on a synthetic neural network with quantized weights, the neuromorphic architecture is trained to achieve the desired computation in simulation and optimized offline to account for the practical constraints of the polymer architecture. The polymer transistors and memristive storage elements of the artificial neural network are emulated in this prototype skin with conventional silicon circuits as an intermediate proof-of-concept as we transition from lithography to polymer printing to produce a skin that exhibits the desired characteristics, enabled by our co-design framework. A limited fraction of a skin sheet.

1   Introduction

Research into alternative structures for robotic devices, such as chemical robots, shape-shifting robots, and massively modular robots has become popular recently due to three motivators: application areas, biological inspiration, and academic interest. In the United States, several government sponsored research programs have focused on the application of providing access to "denied areas" through such novel modalities. Suggested application capabilities include liquid robots that ooze under closed doors and "flow-bots" that can sequentially pass themselves through a small opening to reassemble on the other side. From the perspective of biological inspiration, invertebrates, such as worms, possess novel locomotion schemes from unusual material properties for similar capabilities. In addition, a mouse can deform its body to squeeze through any orifice that its head can fit through. (The skull is the largest rigid member within the body). These are capabilities that seem useful to soft robotic devices and intelligent meta-materials, as well.

© Springer Nature Singapore Pte Ltd. 2016
B. Vinod et al. (Eds.): ICAARS 2016, CCIS 627, pp. 121–137, 2016.
DOI: 10.1007/978-981-10-2845-8_10

Soft robotics is fast emerging for its advantages such as flexibility, safety, etc. One paradigm for soft robotics is the "JamBot" concept. It is a novel form of shape-shifting soft robot that uses "jammable" particles simulating a fluid that flows inside a deformable "balloon" segment [1]. When air of sufficient pressure is present inside the balloon segment, the particles move with respect to one another and the entire segment is deformable. But when the air is evacuated from within the membrane, the particles compress and interlock (jamming together). This makes the segment rigid. "Molecule"-like self-reconfigurable robots [2–4] rely on large numbers of identical rigid particles, each with their own sensing, processing and actuation, to create voxel-like assemblies of structures. Combinations of these jammable or molecule-like segments create programmable matter with new and unfamiliar characteristics. As complex materials advance, design tools for smart systems become increasingly necessary.

Within the Collaborative Robotics Lab, our approach to soft robotics is to create a self-contained robotic system entirely out of non-rigid materials [5], similar in physical embodiment to the approach exemplified by the JamBot. But fundamentally, we want to create highly integrated smart materials from which we can build new types of devices through design paradigms that enable the co-design of structure, sensing, computation and actuation. We call these multi-layered smart meta-materials initially prototyped by shape-deposition manufacturing [6] as Structured Computational Polymers (SCP) [7]. This is a long-term undertaking and the work reported here takes an incremental approach including intermediate forms similar to the Molecule-type embodiments to make use of conventional components.

In addition to its physical structure, a robot requires four additional components: perception, cognition, actuation, and power. Integrating all these capabilities into a functioning entity from soft components is not fully realizable today, but advances in our lab and other labs in organic, printable semiconductors [8], compressible and incompressible fluid-based actuation [9], gel- and liquid-based sensing [10], thin-film batteries and photovoltaics, and multi-material fabrication methodologies will soon make this a reality. The integration of photovoltaics into soft materials can be accomplished using flexible organic solar cells [31]. However, organic solar cells have much lower conversion efficiency than crystalline inorganic solar cells. A promising approach for integrating crystalline inorganic solar cells on flexible substrates is to use the "island-bridge" architecture [32]. An additional advantage of the "island-bridge" architecture is that a common silicon substrate can be shared between the solar cells and electronic circuits for power management and computation [33].

The sub-components we have chosen to base our current work on at this early incremental stage include water hammer based actuation [11], and synthetic neural networks from a CMOL process [12] for distributed cognition, with conventional on-board power sources. As the robotic system has not been fully realized, we describe the results to-date on these subcomponents as well as interim realizations using conventional components for Structured Computational Polymers and Wireless Sensor/Actuator/Control Networks in the following pages.

2   SoftBot Components

As mentioned above, there are five basic components for a robot: perception, cognition, actuation, power and structure. Ultimately, we hope to provide printable polymer solutions which possess all these components. This paper investigates the combination of sensing and cognition embedded into structure.

2.1   Structured Computational Polymers

Structured Computational Polymers (SCP) are what we call a new class of proposed smart materials that represent the combination of perception, cognition, actuation and structure into a "purpose-built" material [7]. An example sheet material of one such meta-material is illustrated in Fig. 1. The proposed material combines perception, cognition and actuation. Pressure sensitive tactels provide the perception, an organic semiconductor neural network provides the cognition (computation), and electrorheological gel [24] within the cells that can electrically modify viscosity provides actuation. For the prototype in this paper, we use shape deposition manufacturing, which builds up materials layer by layer [6], but our long-term plans include mass customization of these purpose-built metamaterials through 3-D printing of both electronics and structure.

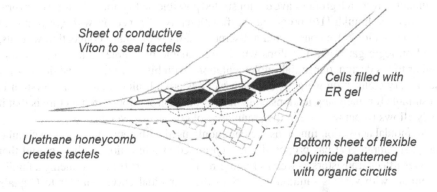

Sheet of conductive
Viton to seal tactels

Cells filled with
ER gel

Urethane honeycomb
creates tactels

Bottom sheet of flexible
polyimide patterned
with organic circuits

Fig. 1. An as yet unrealized example Structured Computational Polymer metamaterial is illustrated that combines sensing, computation and actuation in a generic material. From such a material, pressure-sensitive gloves could be cut and programmed, or a scoring suit for Taekwondo, or a robotic skin, as described later.

In Fig. 1, a generic cognitive architecture is patterned on the bottom substrate, either pre-programmed or learning-enabled. The cells will contain an electrode and detector for the capacitive cell, above. The next layer is the honeycomb of cells, which are molded onto the flexible bottom substrate. A hexagonal array has been chose for this example, but square or triangular arrays are possible. The cells are filled with an electrorheological gel that acts as a dielectric for the capacitive sensing. On the top, a bi-layer of conducting and non-conducting Viton is poured over the sandwich or pre-formed and affixed with adhesive, serving as the top electrode. (Similar to [24]).

2.2 Neuromorphic Architecture

To realize the computational component of SCPs, we use our polymer Synthetic Neural Network (SNN) which is described in [13]. Neuromorphic architectures are designed to mimic information processing similar to biological systems processing and ours is a hardware implementation of an artificial neural network. The key benefits of a biologically-inspired architecture are reduced power consumption, inherent fault-tolerance, generic learning and the foundation for true hardware-based AI.

Artificial neural networks (ANN), being the earliest and most ubiquitous example of neuromorphic architecture, are mathematical constructs that attempt to capture the essential components and functionalities of biological neural networks. They are most often used to model systems where the non-linear relationship is not explicitly known and difficult or impossible to determine analytically. ANNs have been employed in applications such as image processing [14, 26], and handwriting recognition [15] where the system is expected to learn over time. However, their real-time performance can be limited due to emulation on serial machines especially if the system is expected to perform on-line learning.

2.3 Prior Hardware-Based ANNs

A number of research groups have demonstrated possible realizations of hardware neural networks. Deshmukh [16] proposed the functionality of a neuron with conventional CMOS technology. He constructed a discrete neuron with binary connection weights, based on logic gates and flip flops which are capable of simple pattern recognition. Similar to his design, our initial implementations with bistable memristive devices [8] uses binary connection weights, but such weights are a limitation as such a system is not suitable for many applications. A benefit of our neuromorphic architecture is that it easily allows for an increase in the granularity of connection weights.

Sigmoidal activation functions are commonly used with neural networks in simulation [18]. Gupta [17] has proposed a design aimed at realization of the sigmoid that includes fifteen transistors as well as four current sources capable of producing a family of outputs with various saturation levels of the sigmoidal curve. Similar to Gupta's design proposal, our circuit can also obtain a family of activation functions that can approximate a sigmoidal curve and has been realized in organic circuitry. However, our design is only based on a single transistor, which makes it easier to fabricate in a highly redundant, distributed array.

A number of companies, including Intel, IBM, AMD, Hitachi, and Siemens, offer commercial chips based on CMOS technology, that to a various extent (degree of precision, including or excluding learning ability, various network architectures), realize functionality of neural networks [19]. At present our design does not incorporate any learning algorithms. Pre-computed connection weights, via external software training such the Matlab ANN Tool Box, or Emergent, have to be manually imported. Additionally, there is a limit to the precision of both the activation function and the connection weights. The accuracy of activation function is explicitly related to the physical characteristics of the field effect transistor used. The precision of connection weights, however, can be arbitrarily extended using greater quantization levels with more memristive devices.

A device made of molecules and nanoparticles, termed nanoparticle organic memory field-effect transistor, or NOMFET [20], was shown to exhibit a facilitating (excitatory) and depressing (inhibitory) behavior of a biological spiking synapse. Biolek et al. [21] have suggested the possibility of employing a silicon-based memristor to realize the time dependent characteristics of a biological spiking synapse. Their design utilizes metal-oxide semiconductor neurons and silicon based memristors (short for memory resistor) as a synapses for synaptic functions such as spike, time dependent plasticity. In this design, memristors are arranged into a cross-bar with pre and post-synaptic neurons being located on adjacent sides of the cross-bar. This allows for every post-synaptic neuron to receive information from every pre-synaptic neuron. The use of memristive synapses results in neural behavior akin to spiking, biological neurons.

The charge in synapse is directly related to the time dependent input signal. Biology calls this concept as a synaptic plasticity. Lack of stimuli results in synapse de-learning or forgetting stored information. We propose the design, based on the saturation property of organic bi-stable devices. Once synaptic weights are set, during the learning stage, the synapse will retain this information indefinitely. This property makes it much more analogous to conventional ANNs and easier to employ in standard engineering applications [25].

3   Architecture

A biological neuron has a synapse and soma. Synapses are responsible for weighting the chemical or electrical input signal and passing it onto the soma, or neuron body, for further processing [22]. Its purpose is to provide a neuron with an input that is proportional to the importance (weight) of the signal from the outputting neuron that produced it. An input from an "important" neuron is weighted more heavily and is generally accepted that the "learning" is stored in the synaptic weights. Learning (neuro- or synaptic plasticity) is accomplished by modifying, either increasing or decreasing, the strength (weight) of the synapse [27].

In an artificial neuron the functionality of a synapse [28] is realized via a connection weight. Analogously to a biological synapse, connection weight from an "important" neuron is significantly greater than a connection weight from an "unimportant" neuron. Learning in an ANN is accomplished by modifying the numerical value of the aforementioned connection weight.

The function of a soma, in both biological and artificial neurons, is to sum all the input signals and produce an output signal when a predefined threshold value has been exceeded by all these summed inputs. Whereas biological neurons encode the information by modifying the frequency of firing, in artificial neural networks it is the amplitude of the signal that changes.

$$f(x) = \varphi\left(\sum_i (x_i w_i) \right) \qquad (1)$$

Equation 1 represents the algorithm commonly used to compute the output of an artificial neuron. The input (x_i) is multiplied by the connection weight (w_i), which takes place in the synapse. The summation of all the products, $\left(\sum_i (x_i w_i)\right)$, is carried out in the soma and produces an output based on the activation function φ [29]. Additionally, bias values are added to the product of inputs and connection weights. The bias is typically assumed to the zeroth weight with input of one.

A bistable memristive device is a memory device represented by one of two resistor values. It can be in one of two possible states, ON (low resistance) or OFF (high resistance) state. The uniqueness of our work has been to employ organic bistable memristive devices as the synapses for our synthetic neural networks. Figure 2 shows the circuit if a memristor device modeled as two resistors with the symbolic representation of a memristor.

Fig. 2. Memristor circuit and its symbolic representation

In both biological neurons and artificial neurons, the soma performs two functions. First, it sums all of the dendritic inputs and then fires, producing a bounded output proportional to the input. The signal will never exceed the maximum and minimum values (saturation). For an unbounded input there is a bounded output, making this a critical property. A single transistor circuit is used as a soma for summation and

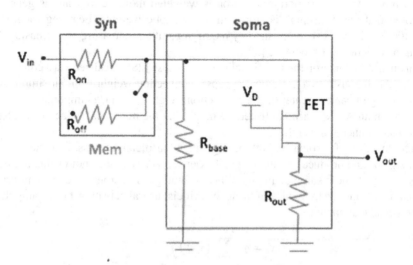

Fig. 3. Schematic of a single neuron with Synapse (Syn) and Soma.

activation. Figure 3 shows the schematic of a single neuron. Mem is the memristor device, which will be represented in a symbol as in Fig. 5, discussed later in this paper.

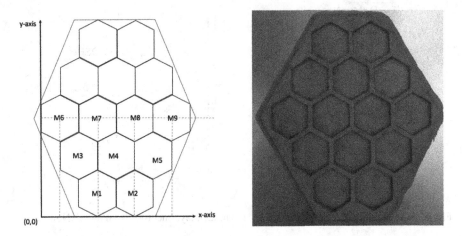

Fig. 4. The hexagonal cells in the SCP were numbered as shown and for simplicity of design and calculation only the named cells were considered.

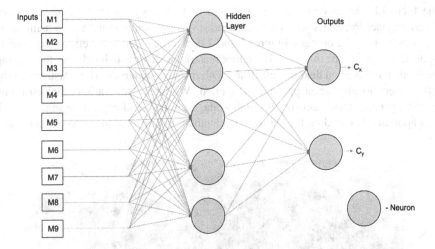

Fig. 5. Synthetic Neural Network architecture with three distinct layers. Input layer has 9 inputs, hidden layer has 5 neurons, and output consists of two neurons. Only neurons in the Hidden layer and Output layer are needed when creating a hardware neural network as neurons in Input layer are only a conceptual representation of inputs (for instance from sensors) to the network.

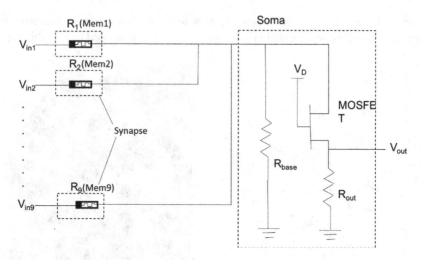

Fig. 6. The 9-input circuit that implements the hidden layer neurons from the SNN in Fig. 4.

4   Embedded Sensing

The focus of this paper is on the co-design methodology for the use of Structured Computational Polymers with embedded sensing and computation. Yet, sensing is an important part of the process. Figures 1 and 7 depict the hexagonal cells as the sensing inputs in our prototype material. The entire material is flexible to handle, so the sensing mechanism is based on flexible cells filled with resistive materials. The resistance of the cell changes locally when pressure is applied. We have used various dielectric and resistive gels for tactile sensing through voltage dividers and capacitive sensing [24]. This approach is based on the sensing mechanism proportional to cross-sectional area

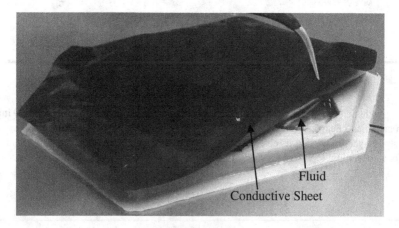

Fig. 7. Prototype of Structured Computational Polymers showing encapsulated resistive fluid in one of the hexagonal cells with conductive electrode pulled back.

of the gel as it squeezes down. The capacitive mechanism requires signal conditioning to convert the capacitive value to a voltage. Collaborators at the Faboratory are developing liquid-metal filled polymer stretchable sensors based on Ga-In solders [23]. This type of sensing mechanism, based on cross-sectional area of the metal as it stretches, is directly compatible with the underlying neuromorphic architecture as well.

5   Co-design of Form and Function

The creation and wide-scale availability of synthetic polymers during and after World War II made an enormous impact on manufacturing and design. As a bulk material, it could be formed into a variety of bar, sheet and ingot shapes (1-D, 2-D and 3-D forms) for many types of conventional and novel forming processes. But the real strength of synthetic polymers was how they expanded the range of materials characteristics from which designers could choose to implement their designs. In a similar vein, the idea behind Structured Computational Polymers is to expand the design space of materials. But polymers only expanded the range of existing characteristics, such as density, Young's modulus, and thermal conductance. Intelligent meta-materials endeavor to expand the types of characteristics at the designer's discretion with such things as sensing, computation and actuation. These new characteristics demand new paradigms of co-design so designers of smart products can harness the full potential of these novel materials.

As described above, the Collaborative Mechatronics Lab is working on integrating the fabrication of neuromorphic architecture for computation, polymer sensors for perception, and 3-D printable structure to create meta-materials for smart product design to move away from the post-attachment of discrete computing, sensing and actuation elements. A critical aspect of this design process is the implementation of embedded algorithms meaningful to the desired functionality of the intended artifact. For our synthetic neural network paradigm, this reduces to the selection of weights in a highly interconnected artificial neural network. These weights are encoded in resistor values in our synthetic neural network and either directly programmed or learned in 'emergent'. The polymer lithography-fabricated SNNs we've created in the lab are programmable in emergent with memristive bistable devices. For this paper, the weights are programmed and fixed at design time.

The functional and algorithmic goal of this flexible robotic skin is to compute a localized centroid of pressure in periodic regions of interest. The design approach can be developed for a specific purpose or in a generic fashion. The biological systems gives us a good approach for purpose-built. The biological neurons are connected from the sensory end to the spin by long nerves running through the body, some do directly go to the brain, Johansson and Vallbo [39]. To prove the concept of combining the sensing, cognition into structure, we chose to develop a purpose-built design.

A neural network is developed for our purpose built design. The network gives the centroid location within the area the network is spread. For this, we had different approaches. One of the approach is to have a node for 14 hexagonal cell as shown in Fig. 4. Another approach would be, to have an output at each cell. Each cell can identify the sensor input at the 6 surrounding cells. The location of these 6 cells are provided in the middle cell. This makes each cell independent to each other, as all cells will be connected to each other. The input pressure at one cell will be passed to 6 cells surrounding it. This provides enormous redundancy. In the paper, the first design approach will be explored in detail. The cognition layer is defined to form nodes for 14 cells.

The initial step before computing the centroid is to define a reference frame and then compute. Equation 2, has been identified to calculate the centroid of 9 cell from the 14 cells shown above, to reduce the complexity. This equation for 9 cells can be extended to 14 cells. The origin is selected by making sure all cells lie in the positive quadrant.

$$C_x = \frac{a(M_6) + 5a(M_2 + M_8) + 2a(M_3) + 4a(M_4)+}{6a(M_5) + 3a(M_1 + M_7) + 7a(M_9)} \bigg/ \sum_i^9 M_i$$

$$C_y = \frac{b(M_1 + M_2) + [(b+1.5) * (M_3 + M_4 + M_5)]+}{[(b+3) * (M_5 + M_6 + M_7 + M_8)]} \bigg/ \sum_i^9 M_i \qquad (2)$$

Where, C_x and C_y refers to the centroid positions along x-axis and y-axis respectively. The centroid, in our case for hexagonal cells, was the intersection of the lines joining the vertex with the mid-point on the other side. 'a' refers to the distance from the origin to the center of the cell closest to any of the x-axis. 'b' refers to the distance from origin to the center of the cell closest to the y-axis. The physical design of the SCP led to values in the equation above where 'a' refers to 0.8 and 'b' refers to 1. By substituting the a, b values in the above equation,

$$C_x = \frac{0.8(M_6) + 4(M_2 + M_8) + 1.6(M_3) + 3.2(M_4)+}{4.8(M_5) + 2.4(M_1 + M_7) + 5.6(M_9)} \bigg/ \sum_i^9 M_i$$

$$C_y = \frac{(M_1 + M_2) + [2.5 * (M_3 + M_4 + M_5)]+}{[4 * (M_5 + M_6 + M_7 + M_8)]} \bigg/ \sum_i^9 M_i \qquad (3)$$

Rather than analytically determine weights from the equation above, which is complex even for this simple example, the neuromorphic architecture is employed as a feature of the co-design framework to learn the appropriate mapping. To do this, we use the above equation to simulate the desired behavior of the meta-material. Then, with the Emergent, a large set of training vectors is first simulated, then fed into the backpropagation training algorithm on a proposed network configuration to generate a vector of weights. A region is defined as an area of nine hexagonal cells, though it would be possible to create a different Structured Computational Polymer with square "tactels," for example.

For the 9 input neural network, it requires to define neurons in the hidden layer. 2 neurons provide the output as location of centroid in 'x' and 'y'. We have tried different number of neurons in the hidden layer. 5 neurons in the hidden layer is the optimized option which gave expected results. To learn the algorithm of the centroid computation, several sets of input matrices with output x and y centroid values were fed to the learning algorithm. The number of neurons in the hidden layer and output layer was varied to explore various network configurations. We started with four fully connected neurons in the hidden layer and two output neurons, then simulated the performance of the cognitive layer. After verifying performance, a hidden layer of five neurons was chosen. Because our neuromorphic architecture is constrained to quantized weight values greater than zero, these constraints must be simulated to ensure optimal operation on the implemented SCP. (This includes the use of a negative offset value in each neuron.) These constraints generally reduce the overall accuracy of the network for any given network size, but increasing the number of neurons in the hidden layer can compensate to produce better accuracy.

The circuit to implement each individual neuron, using the SNN from [2], is shown in Fig. 6.

Given the connection weights (w) and the base resistance value (R_{base}) the input resistance values (R) for each "synapse" can be calculated from the equation:

$$\text{Resistor value (R)} = R_{base}\left(\frac{1-w}{w}\right) \tag{4}$$

The memristor is designed with the resistor value calculated above, which forms the synapse. The equation clearly states that, the resistor value will not be valid if the weights are below zero or above one. So, the constraint on the system is the limits of weights to be 0-1. This constraint is dealt with high priority while training the neural network.

The training of the neural network is the real challenge in this section. This is because of the constraint on the weights. All the weights being positive, proper training is crucial. Initially Matlab is employed to train the network. But, Matlab doesn't provide the flexibility to put constraint on the weights. Emergent software found to be suitable for this application. Emergent software is used to train the neural networks by setting a constraint on the weights.

6 Implementation

The polymer electronics designed to be trapped inside the silicon rubber. This rubber has durometer as 10, which makes the skin more flexible. The neural network designed in the previous section gives the weights for the input resistor. All the components are soldered onto this flex circuit. In this pressure sensitive skin, the amount of pressure applied on the surface of touch is translated by the resistive material in each cell. In our polymer network, memristive bistable devices would implement the memory elements that store the weights. For this prototype implementation, we used conventional silicon components to implement the synapses and somas of each neuron. A silicon MOSFET in analog mode implements the sigmoidal output function to produce the non-linear activation function needed for multi-layer perceptron's.

Different design constructions are defined and laid out onto the flex circuit. This gives the flexibility to cut the sheet as per the required configuration and program the weights to define the resistors. The flex circuit gives flexibility to the skin, making it feel like the real skin. The whole objective of the design is to create a cell with uniform set of circuitry. Then by just replicate the cell into whole bunch of cells, gives endless possibilities to explore. The connections are made on the flex circuit, according to design construction.

From the co-design method, the values of weights were obtained and directly chosen for implementation in the silicon based circuit. Op-amps were employed as non-inverting amplifiers between the cascaded neuronal outputs and inputs to perform impedance matching between layers. Each isolation amplifier had a gain of 2.5 V to maintain operation in the nonlinear working region. A resistive material with a voltage divider of 100 K ohms provided the input signal.

Each cell in the prototype SCP, neighboring with 6 cells, is equipped with a polymer micro sensor and distributed cognition (SNN). Each cell has a copper electrode at the bottom, which is a part of the electronics attached to the skin. The Aloe-Vera gel is filled on the top of the copper inside the cells. The resistivity of the gel is 5–20 kΩ-cm. The net resistance of each cell is a function of the electrode area and distribution of gel between the electrodes as a function of pressure. The entire skin is then covered by a conductive sheet. The conductive sheet has surface resistivity of 30 Ω/□. The experimental setup is built as in Fig. 7.

The experiment is setup with the silicon rubber, filled with Aloe-Vera gel and sealed by the conductive sheet. The sealing of the conductive sheet onto each cell is done by an adhesive, Sil-Poxy. It is a type of adhesive which can allow the silicon or urethane rubber to stick onto other materials. The adhesive requires 12 min cure time, so the bonding takes place. The adhesive material is flexible after cured, which prevents the skin from being rigid. The gel is now trapped inside the cell. When pressure is applied onto the cell, the liquid inside moves towards the walls make a deformed shape. The distance between the conductive sheet and the bottom copper sheet is being reduced. This provides the variable resistance as per the pressure applied onto the surface. The range of resistance provided when no pressure applied to full pressure applied is measured to be 60 kΩ–30 kΩ.

A voltage of 4.2 V is provided to the memristor. The gel and conductive sheet at each cell is a part of the memristor of each input. This divides the voltage as the gel's variable resistance and fed as the input to the circuitry. The electronics provide the location of the cell at the node, forming and intermediate output.

7 Results

This paper describes a prototype of a pressure-sensitive skin developed utilizing a design paradigm for Structured Computational Polymers. Our polymer electronics work has been developed using lithography for patterning the semiconducting devices, including FETs and bistable memristive devices. However, for this prototype, since we have not completed the transition to printing-based polymer electronics necessary for fabrication, we developed this proof of concept sheet meta-material with conventional silicon electronics using pourable urethane and shape-deposition manufacturing techniques.

We cannot duplicate the pressure distributions simulated during the training of the network, but the following results show a limited set of tactels actuated to demonstrate the effectiveness of the skin for pressure sensing as well as the usefulness of the co-design paradigm to effectively implement a specific functionality from a "purpose-built" SCP sheet.

The calculation of centroid for 9 cells is defined in the above sections. This is implemented though neural network, with 5 neurons in the hidden layer and 2 output neurons providing the centroid location. For a set of input combinations, the formula gives the ground-truth values of the location (C_x, C_y). Initially, there is no weight constraint imposed onto the network. The trained neural network gave the simulations results, which has 6 % average error.

Weight constraint is an important metric, as it determines the values of the resistor as discussed with Eq. 4. So, the weights are constrained between 0 and 1. This constraint is fed into the Emergent software and the network is trained. The weights defined after the training data are used to get the simulation results. A comparison between the ground-truth and the simulation results is shown in Figs. 8 and 9, individually for C_x and C_y.

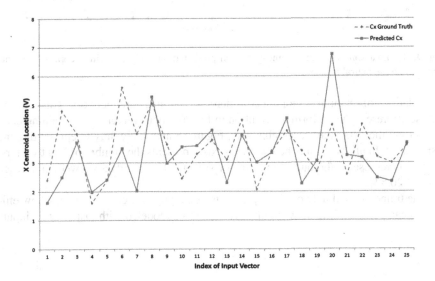

Fig. 8. Comparison between Ground-truth and predicted values of C_x with weight constraints imposed on the neural network.

A data set of 200 input combinations are used to train the neural network. These input vectors are uniformly distributed over the skin. The inputs are considered to be independent and also sets of 2, 3, 4 at a particular instance and the output is recorded. The obtained weights are then feed into a Matlab program to get the predicted values of C_x and C_y. The average error in predicting the location is about 30 %. The minimum error is 2.5 % and the maximum error is 59 %. To provide the better understanding of how the error is behaving, the median is also calculated, 27.5 %. The average error percentage is considerably high compared to the network without any constraints. The training data plays an important role in error existence. But the weight constraint which required all the weights in the network to be positive, contributes to the error.

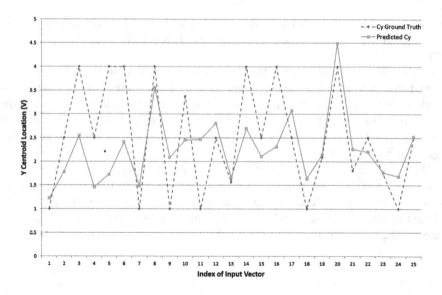

Fig. 9. Comparison between Ground-truth and predicted values of C_y with weight constraints imposed on the neural network.

A data set of 28 input vector are considered to test the neural network. This reduced data set represent the uniform distribution of the 200 input vectors in the training data, to interpret the data in an acceptable way. Figures 8 and 9, are drawn representing the test data set. In all the figures below, the x-axis represents the number of input vectors, the y-axis represents the output in terms of voltage. The test data showed an average error of 20.5 %.

The trained neural network is implemented on a physical circuit to check how efficient it can perform. The network discussed so far is modeled with just 2 active inputs

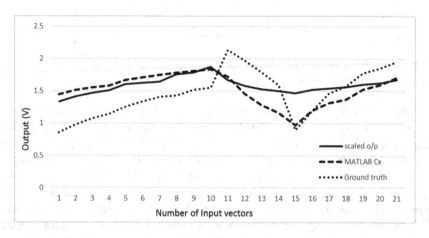

Fig. 10. C_x Values of Ground-truth Vs Predicted Output Vs measured Physical Output for 2 of the inputs tested.

in emergent in a similar fashion as the 9 input network described above. The ground-truth values are calculated using the formula. Trained neural network provides the predicted values for the output for C_x. The weights determined from the emergent are converted to the resistor values using the Eq. 4 and then the circuit is implemented. The pressure sensitive sensor provided the variance in the resistance as per the pressure applied. This input is fed to the network and the outputs are registered. The comparison between the ground-truth, predicted and the physical outputs is shown in the Fig. 10.

The average error is about 23 % with a minimum error as 0.5 % and maximum error as 63.5 %. The error is in acceptable range, this error exists because of the biased in the modeled network. Bias is not implemented in the physical circuit. Once we have a good results with the 2 active inputs network, it can be expanded to the 9 input-2 output network. This requires, comparatively, larger network to accommodate more inputs and the neurons in the hidden layer and the output. For this, we employed the flex circuit as discussed in previous sections.

The error encountered in the physical output when 2 inputs are tested, is under and acceptable range. As per the error in predicted output for the 9 input network, we can conclude that the average error to be under the acceptable range. These weights can be used to implement the complete circuit for the all the 9 inputs. This can be efficiently achieved by printing on a flex circuit sheet, as discussed earlier.

8 · Conclusion

The results show that for the selected cells, the skin matches the predicted values with an average error under the acceptable range. This indicates that the desired capability of using the pressure-sensitive SCP to compute the centroid of pressure was appropriately co-designed, based on the stated goals. Pressure was sensed accurately by using the distributed sensors of the soft skin and the distributed computation.

Printing of these components in a more uniform way and this co-design technique is extended to larger sizes and to different form factors (1-D, 2-D and 3-D). Rapid prototyping of these materials through enhanced 3-D printing techniques will increase the number of neurons that can be incorporated into the hidden layer thereby enhancing the results of the learning algorithm, to deal with the weight constraints.

The concept of integrating the perception by sensing the pressure, cognition with the neuromorphic architecture and structure using flexible polymer meta-materials is evaluated. This is clearly demonstrated by the soft skin developed and the results along with the average error percentage is presented in this paper.

Acknowledgements. The authors wish to thank Rebecca Kramer for helpful comments on the document. This work was partially supported by the NSF through grant 1450342-CNS by the NSF Center for Robots and Sensors for the Human Well-Being (RoSeHUB), and by the Purdue Robotics Accelerator.

References

1. Steltz, E., Mozeika, A., Rodenberg, N., Brown, E.: JSEL: jamming skin enabled locomotion. In: 2009 IEEE/RSJ International Conference on Intelligent Robots and Systems, pp. 5672–5677, October 2009

2. Butler, Z., Kotay, K., Rus, D., Tomita, K.: Generic decentralized control for lattice-based self-reconfigurable robots. Int. J. Rob. Res. **23**(9), 919–937 (2004)

3. Butler, Z., Rus, D.: Distributed motion planning for 3D modular robots with unit-compressible modules. In: Boissonnat, J.-D., Burdick, J., Goldberg, K., Hutchinson, S. (eds.) Algorithmic Foundations of Robotics V. Springer Tracts in Advanced Robotics, vol. 7, pp. 435–451. Springer, Heidelberg (2005)

4. Fitch, R., Butler, Z.: Million module March: scalable locomotion for large self reconfiguring robots. Int. J. Rob. Res. **27**(3–4), 331–343 (2008)

5. Trivedi, D., Rahn, D., Kier, M., Walker, D.: Soft robotics: Biological inspiration, state of the art, and future research. J. Appl. Bionics Biomech. **5**(3), 99–117 (2008)

6. Hatanaka, M., Cutkosky, M.R.: Process planning for embedding flexible materials in multi-material prototypes. In: ASME 2003 International Design Engineering Technical Conferences and Computers and Information in Engineering Conference, Chicago, USA, 2–6 September 2003

7. Nawrocki, R.A., Yang, X., Shaheen, S.E., Voyles, R.M.: Structured computational polymers for a soft robot: actuation and cognition. In: IEEE International Conference on Robotics and Automation, pp. 5115–5122, April 2011

8. Nawrocki, R.A., Voyles, R.M., Shaheen, S.E.: Neurons in polymer: hardware neural units based on polymer memristive devices and polymer transistors. IEEE Trans. Electron Devices **61**(10), 3513–3519 (2014)

9. Yang, X., Voyles, R.M., Li K., Povilus, S.: Experimental comparison of robotics locomotion with passive tether and active tether. In: IEEE Workshop on Safety, Security and Rescue Robots, Denver, CO, November 2009

10. Paik, J.K., Kramer, R.K., Wood, R.J.: Stretchable circuits and sensors for robotic origami. In: IEEE International Conference on Intelligent Robotics and Systems, San Francisco USA (2011)

11. Perrin, D.P., Kwon, A., Howe, R.D.: A novel actuated tether design for rescue robots using hydraulic transients. In: 2004 Proceedings of the 2004 IEEE International Conference on Robotics and Automation, ICRA 2004, 26 April 26–1 May 2004, vol. 4, pp. 3482–3487 (2004)

12. Strukov, D.B., Likharev, K.K.: Prospects for the development of digital CMOL circuits. In: IEEE International Symposium on Nanoscale Architectures, NANOARCH 2007, pp. 109–116 (2007)

13. Nawrocki, R.A., Shaheen, S.E., Voyles, R.M.: A neuromorphic architecture from single transistor neurons with organic bistable devices for weights. In: International Joint Conference on Neural Networks (IJCNN), pp. 450–456 (2011)

14. Kandel, E.R., Schwartz, J.H., Jessel, T.M.: Principles of Neural Science, pp. 832–850. McGraw-Hill, New York (2000)

15. Likharev, K.K., Mayr, A., Muckra, I., Türel, Ö.: CrossNets: high-performance neuromorphic architectures for CMOL circuits. Ann. N.Y. Acad. Sci. **146–163**, 2003 (1006)

16. Deshmukh, A., Morghade, J., Khera, A., Bajaj, P.: Binary Neural Networks–A CMOS Design Approach. In: Khosla, R., Howlett, R.J., Jain, L.C. (eds.) Knowledge-Based Intelligent Information and Engineering Systems. LNCS, vol. 3681, pp. 1291–1296. Springer, Heidelberg (2005)

17. Gupta, A.K., Bhat, N.: Asymmetric cross-coupled differential pair configuration to realize neuron activation function and its derivative. IEEE Trans. Circui. Syst. II-Express Briefs **52**(1), 10–13 (2005)
18. Haykin, S.: Neural Networks: A Comprehensive Foundation. Prentice Hall, Upper Saddle River (1999)
19. Strukov, D.B., Snider, G.S., Stewart, D.R., Williams, R.S.: The missing memristor found. Nature **453**, 80–83 (2008)
20. Türel, Ö., Lee, J.H., Ma, X., Likharev, K.K.: Neuromorphic architectures for nanoelectronic circuits. Int. J. Circuit Theory Appl. **23**, 277–302 (2004)
21. Biolek, D., Biolek, Z., Biolkova, V.: SPICE modeling of memristive, memcapacitive, and meminductive systems. In: Proceedings of ECCTD 2009, European Conference on Circuit Theory and Design, Antalya, Turkey pp. 249–252 (2009)
22. Atallah, H.E., Frank, M.J., O'Reilly, R.C.: Hippocampus, cortex, and basal ganglia: Insights from computational models of complementary learning systems. Neurobiol. Learn. Mem. **82**, 253–267 (2004)
23. Park, Y.L., Majidi, C., Kramer, R.K., Berard, P., Wood, R.J.: Hyperelastic pressure sensing with a liquid-embedded elastomer. J. Micromech. Microeng. **20**(12), 125029 (2010)
24. Voyles, R.M., Jr., Fedder, G., Khosla, P.K.: Design of a modular tactile sensor and actuator based on an electrorheological gel. In: Proceedings of 1996 IEEE International Conference on Robotics and Automation, Minneapolis, MN, pp. 13–17, April 1996
25. King, J.G., Hines, M., Hill, S., Goodman, P.H., Markram, H., Schurmann, F.: A component-based extension framework for large-scale parallel simulations in NEURON. Front. Neuroinf. (2009)
26. Danchenko, P., Lifshits, F., Orion, I., Koren, S., Solomon, A.D., Mark, S.: NNIC–neural network image compressor for satellite positioning system. Acta Astronaut. **60**(8–9), 622–630 (2007)
27. Nawrocki, R.A., Voyles, R.M., Shaheen, S.E.: Simulating hardware neural networks with organic memristors and organic field effect transistors. In: Proceedings of ANNIE (2010)
28. Alibart, F., Pleutin, S., Guerin, D.: An organic nanoparticle transistor behaving as a biological spiking synapse. Adv. Funct. Mater. **20**, 330–337 (2010)
29. Jo, S.H., Chang, T., Ebong, I., Bhadviya, B.B., Mazumder, P., Lu, W.: Nanoscale memristor device as synapse in neuromorphic systems. Nano Lett. **10**(4), 1297–1301 (2010)
30. Johansson, R.S., Vallbo, A.B.: Tactile sensibility in the human hand: relative and absolute densities of four types of mechanoreceptive units in glabrous skin. J. Physiol. **286**(1), 283–300 (1979)
31. Kaltenbrunner, M., White, M.S., Głowacki, E.D., Sekitani, T., Someya, T., Sariciftci, N.S., Bauer, S.: Ultrathin and lightweight organic solar cells with high flexibility. Nat. Commun. **3**, 770 (2012)
32. Lee, J., Jian, W., Shi, M., Yoon, J., Park, S.-I., Li, M., Liu, Z., Huang, Y., Rogers, J.A.: Stretchable GaAs photovoltaics with designs that enable high areal coverage. Adv. Mater. **23**(8), 986–991 (2011)
33. Pour, G.M., Benyhesan, M.K., Leon-Salas, W.D.: Energy harvesting using substrate photodiodes. IEEE Trans. Circuits Syst. II Express Briefs **61**(7), 501–505 (2014)

Tele-Operation

A Method of Blindfolded Opening of a Door in High Radiation Areas Using a Compliance Controlled Tele-Robot

Tumapala Teja Swaroop$^{(\boxtimes)}$, Surendra Singh Saini, Ushnish Sarkar, and Debasish Datta Ray

Division of Remote Handling and Robotics, Bhabha Atomic Research Centre, Mumbai 400 085, India
{tejswrp, sainiss, ushinish, dray}@barc.gov.in

Abstract. Simultaneous force and Position control is indispensable for the execution of any real world task. In this work, we have investigated the task of opening a door in a hot-cell i.e. high radiation environment with the specified objective of safe completion of task without using a force torque sensor. For this, a compliance control methodology has been formulated which generates both position path and force profile for the task undertaken. The control action employed in the current approach involves position and force control of the manipulator in mutually orthogonal directions viz., radial and tangential directions to the centre of rotation of the door. The kinematic parameters required for such tasks are position of the door's knob and its hinge. The performance of the control algorithm has been tested on a simulated generic robot dynamic model. Firstly, the algorithm and control action was tested for the task of opening the door whose kinematics was known a priori and eventually tested for the task where the prior knowledge of the door kinematics and hinge position was not known.

Keywords: Door opening · Tele-Robot · Compliance control · Hybrid position/force control

1 Introduction

Compliant motion tasks involve interaction forces between the tool and the work piece and demand certain amounts of compliance at either the tool or at the work piece. When contact occurs, the interaction forces limit or modify the free space motion in some manner. Such tasks where the interaction forces must be accommodated rather than resisted are known as compliant motion tasks. The task of opening a door – or a drawer comes under this category and for achieving this task, the manipulator has to deal with several uncertainties associated with the dynamics and kinematics of the door. Hence the use of only position control is not sufficient. For accommodating the interaction forces, the force controller plays a vital role in limiting the contact forces between end effector and the door knob to a zero/minimal desired value. The door opening problem can be considered as a position/force control problem in which the robot workspace can be divided into mutually orthogonal subspaces namely position and force controlled subspaces [1]. The uncertainties involved in manipulation of

© Springer Nature Singapore Pte Ltd. 2016
B. Vinod et al. (Eds.): ICAARS 2016, CCIS 627, pp. 141–152, 2016.
DOI: 10.1007/978-981-10-2845-8_11

opening a door [2] can be divided into two main categories namely: (a) uncertainties related to the dynamic model of the door's inertia, dynamics of the hinge mechanism and (b) uncertainties related to the kinematic model of the door's mechanism prismatic/revolute, location of the hinge and size of the door.

In this paper, we considered a simulated robot dynamic model [3] and simulated kinematic door model which is assumed to be planar and following an arc, for testing the effectiveness of the compliance control algorithm and hybrid position/force controller. Also, the task of opening the door is done by controlling the door angle with respect to the hinge axis.

2 Related Work

In [5], experiments on door opening with a manipulator were performed under the assumption of known door model. The idea of using compliance control for estimating the position path and force profile for a given task and hybrid position/force controller methodology for performing given task has been inspired from [6]. Several velocity – based estimation techniques have also been proposed. References [4, 7] uses adaptive Force/velocity control for opening unknown doors using wrist Force/Torque sensor. For high radiation level environments (likely for most applications of Department of Atomic Energy, Government of India), Force/Torque sensors cannot be deployed at the end effector for measuring interaction forces. In this case, the measurement of inter-action forces of the end-effector of the robot with the environment is achieved indi-rectly by measuring the motor currents. The basis of this approach and its analysis can be found in [8].

3 Compliance Control: Principle and Methodology

In this work, the compliant motion for opening the door has been executed by Hybrid Position/Force Controller. This scheme has been simulated for a 6 degree of freedom robot manipulator for opening the door. The concept of Hybrid controller followed by a scheme of its software simulation is presented in subsequent sections.

3.1 Hybrid Controller

The hybrid position/force controller develops position control torques and force control torques in specified degrees of freedom and makes the manipulator to perform the required task. The objective here is to control the manipulator to achieve smooth interaction with door environment, and to manipulate it in order to complete the task of opening the door.

The Hybrid position/force controller for this task deals with:

- Position Control of a manipulator along the tangential direction to the centre of rotation of the door in which natural force constraints exists,

- Force Control of a manipulator along the radial direction to the centre of rotation of the door in which natural position constraints exists,
- A scheme to implement the mixing of these modes along orthogonal degrees of freedom.

The conceptual schema of Hybrid controller for this task is shown in Fig. 1.

In Fig. 1, θ_a, X_a, Ψ_a, Ψ_d describes the actual joint angles, actual position & orientation, actual door's knob position in Spherical co-ordinates and desired door's knob position in spherical co-ordinates respectively. $\delta\theta_s$, δX_{es}, $\delta\Psi_e$, and $\delta\Psi_{es}$ are the vectors describing joint angle errors, positional errors in selected degrees of freedom, error in door's knob position in spherical co-ordinates and error in door's knob position in spherical co-ordinates in selected degrees of freedom respectively. τ_p is a vector describing the required torques to be given to the corresponding joints for position control.

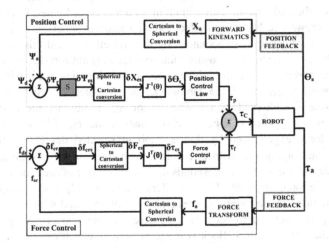

Fig. 1. Hybrid position/force control scheme

τ_a, f_a, f_{ar} and f_{dr} are vectors describing the actual joint torques of the robot, actual force experienced by the end effector, actual force experienced by the end effector/door's knob in terms of spherical co-ordinates and desired force that should be experienced by end effector/door's knob in spherical co-ordinates respectively. δf_{er}, δf_{ers}, δF_{es}, $\delta\tau_{es}$ and τ_f are vectors describing the force error of an end effector/door's knob in spherical co-ordinates, force error of an end effector/door's knob in selected degrees of freedom, Force error of end effector in Cartesian frame, joint torque errors corresponding to the required force control in selected degrees of freedom and required torques to be given to the corresponding joints for force control respectively. It should be mentioned here that the dimension of all the aforementioned vectors are equal to the number of degrees of freedom of the serial mechanism to be controlled.

The position control block and force control block constitutes the architecture of the Controller. In the Position Control block, Ψ_d (azimuth, elevation, R) represents the desired door's knob position in spherical co-ordinates. Ψ_a (azimuth, elevation, R) represents the actual door's knob position in spherical co-ordinates. The matrices S, $S^\perp$ are Selection matrices [9] introduced to decouple Position/Force in orthogonal dimensions. Once the door's knob position error matrix is multiplied with S, the vector $\delta\Psi_{es}$ (door's knob positional error in selected degrees of freedom) is obtained. These positional errors in spherical form will then be converted into Positional errors in Cartesian form δX_{es} (δx, δy, δz, $\delta\alpha$, $\delta\beta$, $\delta\gamma$). δX_{es} represents error in position (δx, δy, δz) and error in orientation ($\delta\alpha$, $\delta\beta$, $\delta\gamma$) in Cartesian frame. The positional errors, in turn, can be related to individual joint angle errors ($\delta\theta_s$) through the Inverse Jacobian (J^{-1}) [1] of the robot. Each element of $\delta\theta_s$ corresponds to the position error of each joint and is given to the respective position controller (PI-Controller) of that joint [7]. The position controller of each joint produces the necessary torques and this will be added with the output of the corresponding force controller and then given to the corresponding motor drive.

Similarly in Force Control block, f_{dr} represents the desired force that should be experienced by the end effector/door's knob in spherical co-ordinates, f_{ar} represents the actual force experienced by the end effector/door's knob in spherical co-ordinates and f_a represents the actual force experienced by the end effector and this is obtained by calculating the end effector force using joint torques τ_a (joint torques are obtained by measuring the currents [9] in the joint motors and multiplying them with the corresponding Torque Constant of the motor). f_{ar} is calculated by converting f_a from Cartesian frame to spherical frame. The vector δf_{er} represents the error in force experienced by door's knob in spherical co-ordinate frame. δf_{ers} (the vector describing the error in force experienced by door's knob in selected degrees of freedom) is obtained by multiplying δf_{er} with $S^\perp$. It is known that $\tau = J^T F$ therefore, we have $\tau_{es} = J^T f_{es}$. Each element of τ_{es} corresponds to the torque error of each joint and is given to the respective force controller (PI-Controller) of that joint [7]. The force controller of each joint produces the necessary torques and this will be added with the output of the corresponding position controller and then given to the corresponding drive. The feedback to the Force Control Block is the joint torques which can be mapped to the currently applied force through the Force transform [10] as:

$$f_a = \left[J^T\right]^{-1} X\tau_a \qquad (1)$$

3.2 Software Simulation of Compliance Control Algorithm

Tasks like opening a door whose kinematic parameters are known/unknown have different input arguments which will be given as inputs to Compliance control algorithm and then the algorithm partitions the degrees of freedom and generates Position path and Force profile. It is then the responsibility of Hybrid Position/Force Controller to make the manipulator to follow the given position path and force profile. The ingredients for the simulation viz., the algorithm flow, the door kinematics and lastly the Robot kinematic and dynamic model, have been presented in the subsequent sections.

Table 1. Link & joint parameters of the simulated robot manipulator

Joints	α_i(degrees)	A_i (m)	D_i(m)	θ_i (degrees)
1	90	0	0	θ_1
2	0	0.4318	0	θ_2
3	−90	0.0203	0.15005	θ_3
4	90	0	0.4318	θ_4
5	−90	0	0	θ_5
6	0	0	0	θ_6

3.3 Robotic Kinematic and Dynamic Model

The robot manipulator model described in [3], are used for computer simulations. The link and joint parameters of the robot model used in this work are given in Table 1.

The dynamic model of the robot is described by set of Euler – Lagrangian equations as follows:

$$M(\theta)\ddot{\theta} + V\left(\theta, \dot{\theta}\right) + G(\theta) + \tau_r(\theta, \tau) = \tau \tag{2}$$

Where, θ, $\dot{\theta}$ and $\ddot{\theta} \in R^6$ be the joint position, velocity and acceleration vectors respectively.

$M(\theta) \in R^{6 \times 6}$ – Mass matrix of the manipulator and positive definite matrix $\forall \theta \in R^6$,

$V\left(\theta, \dot{\theta}\right) \in R^6$ denotes Centrifugal and Coriolis terms,

G ($G(\theta) \in R^6$) is the gravity force vector.

τ_r - torque experienced by manipulator because of the compliant motion.

τ - joint input torque vector.

3.4 Door Modelling and Estimation of Kinematic Parameters

The basic type of motion of door is assumed to be planar and following an arc. Door rotation is modeled by a rotational spring and a damper with governing equations $F_s = -k\theta_{door}$ and $F_d = -c\dot{\theta}_{door}$ respectively. Where k is spring constant expressed in Newton per radians and c is damper constant expressed in Newton second per radians.

$$r^2 = (x - h)^2 + (y - k)^2 \tag{3}$$

Where, (h, k) is the center of rotation of the door and r is the radius of the door with respect to the point of contact with the gripper (x, y).

For estimating the radius and centre of rotation of the door [11], the Eq. (3) can be rewritten as:

$$x^2 + y^2 = r^2 - h^2 - k^2 + 2xh + 2yk \tag{4}$$

The above equation can be expressed in matrix form as: AX = B, where

$$A = [1 \quad x \quad y], B = [x^2 + y^2] \text{ and } X = \begin{bmatrix} r^2 - h^2 - k^2 \\ 2h \\ 2k \end{bmatrix}$$

Moore–Penrose pseudo inverse is then performed for solving X. The value of X is calculated by using Eq. (5).

$$X = (A^T A)^{-1} A^T B \tag{5}$$

X is used for solving the parameters (h, k) and r.

These initial estimated door kinematic parameters are then used by compliance control algorithm for generating the initial position set point and desired interaction forces with the environment. According to the position set point the position controller block of hybrid controller moves the end effector of the robot and eventually door from initial position to the estimated position. During this operation, the forces and moments experienced by the end effector due to any incorrect motion of the manipulator will be taken care by force controller block. The end effector's current position in spherical co-ordinate frame (**azimuth, elevation, R**) is considered for estimating the position of the door. The knowledge about the door's current state can be obtained by monitoring the azimuth value of the current position of the end effector.

If azimuth = 0 ° – Door closed

azimuth ≥ 90 ° – Door opened

If azimuth angle is not greater than 90 °, the current position of the end effector is used again for estimating the new kinematic parameters of the door. The complete process of estimating the door kinematic parameters and the task of opening the door is depicted in the below flow chart (Fig. 2).

3.5   Simulation Scheme

A consolidated block level description for the simulated system is shown in Fig. 3 which illustrates the simulation process of opening a door which is in X – Y Plane.

In Eq. (2), the value τ_r is given by:

$$\tau_r = J^T(\theta) \times F_r \tag{6}$$

F_r – Total force between the manipulator and the kinematic mechanism (door).

F_{sc} – Reaction Force on robot due to door's spring action in Cartesian co – ordinate frame

F_{dc} – Reaction Force on the robot due to door's damping action in Cartesian co – ordinate frame.

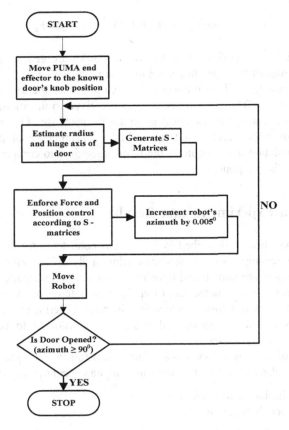

Fig. 2. Flow chart of compliant motion for the task of opening a door

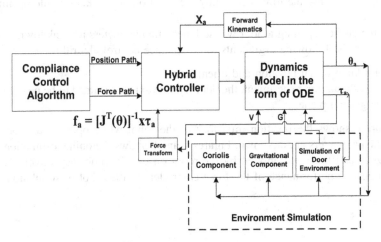

Fig. 3. Computer simulation of compliance control algorithm

$$F_r = -(sgn|r' - r|)X(J^T(\theta))^{-1}\tau_a + F_{sc} + F_{dc} \qquad (7)$$

As shown in Fig. 3, position path and force profiles are generated by the Compliance Control Algorithm depending upon the task input. These paths and profiles are then given as inputs to the hybrid controller which generates the torques required for the manipulator joints. These generated torques are given to the simulated dynamics model of the robot. The dynamics model generates the response of the manipulator (as the achieved joint angles and joint torques) under the influence of the given input torques. The simulation also calculates the torques required to compensate for gravitational and coriolis components.

4 Simulation Experiments and Results

Environment simulation as described in Sect. 3.4 is considered for the present study. The tasks to be accomplished for this simulation study are opening a door whose kinematic parameters are known and opening a door whose kinematic parameters are unknown. The robot manipulator has to apply a zero force on door's knob while opening the door. Without loss of generality, in these experiments the door's knob position in both closed and in opened position is considered to be in reachable workspace without singularities.

For the task of opening a door whose kinematic parameters are known a prior, the user should input the following arguments to compliance control algorithm:

- Door's knob initial position and orientation,
- Equation of Door's hinge axis.

The Compliance Control Algorithm with the above mentioned inputs then generate position path and force profile for completing the task. Figure 4 shows the position trajectory of the robot while opening a door whose kinematic parameters are known a prior. Figure 5 shows the force applied by the robot on door's knob while opening the door.

For the task of opening a door whose kinematic parameters are unknown, the user should input the following arguments to compliance control algorithm:

- Door's knob initial position and orientation,
- For this simulation experiment, the door's hinge axis is assumed to be perpendicular to the ground plane.

Figure 6 shows the position trajectory of the robot while opening a door whose kinematic parameters are unknown. Figures 7 and 8 shows the online estimation of the door radius and the force applied by the robot on door's knob respectively. Table 2 summarizes the performance of the force controller for the robot in simulation.

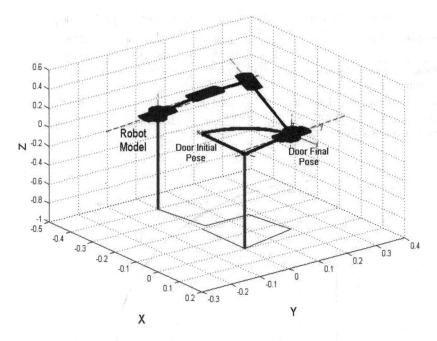

Fig. 4. Position path of the robot while opening a door

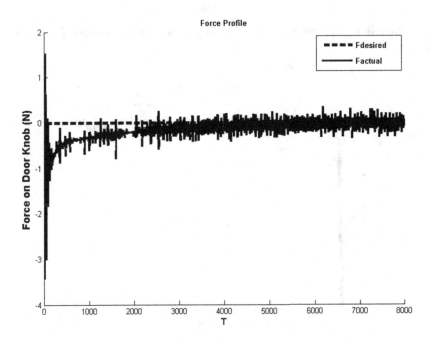

Fig. 5. Force applied by the robot on Door's knob

Table 2. Performance of force controller for the task of opening a door

Illustrative Task	Peak force (N)	Mean force error (N)	Mean force settling (sec)
Opening a door whose kinematic parameters are known[a]	4.80	1.20	0.28
Opening a door whose kinematic parameters are unknown[a]	2.68	1.68	0.42

[a]Prescribed Force = 0 N

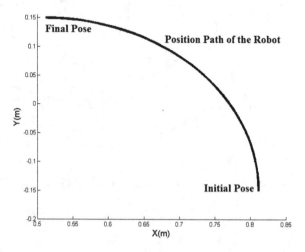

Fig. 6. Position Path of the robot while opening a door whose kinematic parameters are unknown

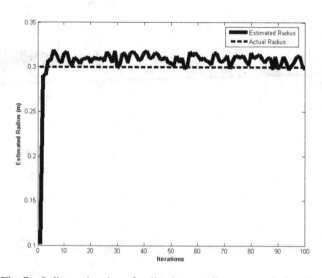

Fig. 7. Online estimation of radius by compliance control algorithm

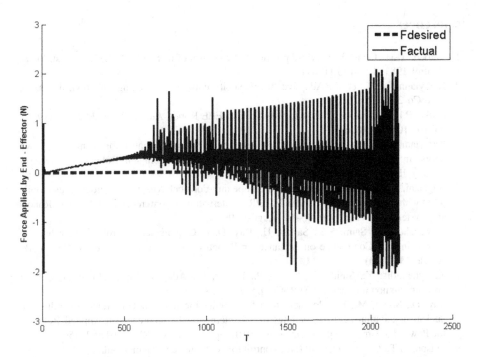

Fig. 8. Force applied by the robot on door's knob while opening a door whose kinematic parameters are unknown

5 Conclusion

The door opening task is not only fundamental from the point of view of modern day environments, but is also representative tasks where motion and force constraints are inherent in the environment structure. This paper presents a Compliance Control based approach for executing the task of opening a door in simulation. Various similar works have been done by using force torque sensors. However, presently, no force torque sensor with radiation resistance capabilities is available. This signifies that, for such tasks in actual hot cell scenario, we have to measure the interaction forces of the robot indirectly using motor currents. In this work, the feasibility and methodology of such a force torque sensor less scheme has been successfully demonstrated. The simulation results are encouraging for going further with the experimental validation of the proposed control scheme in an actual hot-cell on a Tele-Robot developed in-house.

References

1. Raibert, M.H., Craig, J.J.: Hybrid position/force control of manipulators. J. Dyn. Syst. Meas. Control **1981**, 126–133 (1987)
2. Karayiannidis, Y., et al.: Adaptive force/velocity control for opening unknown doors. In: SyRoCo 2012 (2012)
3. Corke, P.I.: A robotics toolbox for MATLAB. IEEE Robot. Autom. Mag. **3**, 24–32 (1996). doi:10.1109/100.486658
4. Karayiannidis, Y., et al.: Open sesame! adaptive force/velocity control for opening unknown doors. In: 2012 IEEE/RSJ International Conference on Intelligent Robots and Systems (IROS). IEEE (2012)
5. Nagatani, K., Yuta, S.: An experiment on opening-door-behavior by an autonomous mobile robot with a manipulator. In: 1995 IEEE/RSJ International Conference on Intelligent Robots and Systems 95, vol. 2, pp. 45–50, August 1995
6. Tumapala, T.S., Saini, S.S., Sarkar, U., Ray, D.D.: Compliance control of tele-robot. In: Proceedings of Conference on Advances in Robotics (AIR 2013), p. 7. ACM, New York, Article 33 (2013)
7. Karayiannidis, Y., Smith, C., Ögren, P., Kragic, D.: Adaptive force/velocity control for opening unknown doors. In: SyRoCo, pp. 753–758 (2012)
8. Ray, D., Singh, M.: Development of a force reflecting tele–robot for remote handling in nuclear installations. In: Proceedings of 1st International Conference on Applied Robotics for Power Industry, Montreal, pp. 1–6 (2010). doi:10.1109/CARPI.2010.5624456
9. Mason, M.T.: Compliance and force control for computed control manipulators, IEEE Trans. Syst. Man Cybern. **1981**, 418–432 (1981). doi:10.1109/TSMC.1981.4308708
10. Ohishi, K., Miyazaki, M., Fujita, M.: Hybrid control of force and position without force sensor. In: Proceedings of IECON 1992, vol. 2, p. 670 (1992). doi:10.1109/IECON.1992.254552
11. Peterson, L., Austin, D., Kragic, D.: High-level control of a mobile manipulator for door opening. In: Proceedings. 2000 IEEE/RSJ International Conference on Intelligent Robots and Systems, IROS 2000, vol. 3. IEEE (2000)

Author Index

Printed in the United States
By Bookmasters